Rhea Almeida
Editor

Transformations of Gender and Race: Family and Developmental Perspectives

Transformations of Gender and Race: Family and Developmental Perspectives has been co-published simultaneously as *Journal of Feminist Family Therapy*, Volume 10, Number 1 1998.

Pre-publication
REVIEWS,
COMMENTARIES,
EVALUATIONS . . .

"**R**hea Almeida and her collaborators are to be commended for this insightful collection of papers. The authors bring us to a deeper level of understanding of the painful, intertwined experiences of racism, classism, sexism, and heterosexism to inform and, indeed, transform clinical practice. Their passionate voices rally us all to press for social justice in the larger society."

Froma Walsh, PhD
Co-Director
Chicago Center for Family Health
Author, Strengthening Family Resilience

Transformations of Gender and Race: Family and Developmental Perspectives

Transformations of Gender and Race: Family and Developmental Perspectives has been co-published simultaneously as *Journal of Feminist Family Therapy*, Volume 10, Number 1 1998.

Transformations of Gender and Race: Family and Developmental Perspectives

Rhea V. Almeida
Editor

Transformations of Gender and Race: Family and Developmental Perspectives has been co-published simultaneously as *Journal of Feminist Family Therapy*, Volume 10, Number 1 1998.

The Haworth Press, Inc.
New York • London • Oxford

Transformations of Gender and Race: Family and Developmental Perspectives has been co-published simultaneously as *Journal of Feminist Family Therapy* ™, Volume 10, Number 1 1998.

The development, preparation, and publication of this work has been undertaken with great care. However, the publisher, employees, editors, and agents of The Haworth Press and all imprints of The Haworth Press, Inc., including The Haworth Medical Press® and Pharmaceutical Products Press®, are not responsible for any errors contained herein or for consequences that may ensue from use of materials or information contained in this work. Opinions expressed by the author(s) are not necessarily those of The Haworth Press, Inc.

The Haworth Press, Inc., 10 Alice Street, Binghamton, NY 13904-1580 USA

Cover design by Thomas J. Mayshock Jr.

Library of Congress Cataloging-in-Publication Data

Transformations of gender and race : family and developmental perspectives / Rhea V. Almeida, editor.
     p. cm.
    "Co-published simultaneously as Journal of feminist family therapy, v. 10, no. 1, 1998."
    Includes bibliographical references and index.
    ISBN 0-7890-0655-3 (alk. paper) – ISBN 0-7890-0673-1
    1. Feminist therapy. 2. Family psychotherapy–Political aspects. 3. Masculinity. 4. Child psychology. 5. Family–Mental health. 6. Minorities–Mental health services. 7. Discrimination in mental health services. 8. Sexism in mental health services. I. Almeida, Rhea V. II. Journal of feminist family therapy, v. 10, no. 1.

RC489.F45T7 1998
616.89–dc21
                                        98-48952
                                            CIP

INDEXING & ABSTRACTING

Contributions to this publication are selectively indexed or abstracted in print, electronic, online, or CD-ROM version(s) of the reference tools and information services listed below. This list is current as of the copyright date of this publication. See the end of this section for additional notes.

- *Abstracts of Research in Pastoral Care & Counseling,* Loyola College, 7135 Minstrel Way, Suite 101, Columbia, MD 21045

- *Alternative Press Index,* Alternative Press Center, Inc., P.O. Box 33109, Baltimore, MD 21218-0401

- *Applied Social Sciences Index & Abstracts (ASSIA) (Online: ASSI via Data-Star) (CDRom: ASSIA Plus),* Bowker-Saur Limited, Maypole House, Maypole Road, East Grinstead, West Sussex RH19 1HH, England

- *CNPIEC Reference Guide: Chinese National Directory of Foreign Periodicals,* P.O. Box 88, Beijing, People's Republic of China

- *Contemporary Women's Issues,* Responsive Databases Services, 23611 Chagrin Boulevard, Suite 320, Beachwood, OH 44122

- *Family Studies Database (online and CD/ROM),* National Information Services Corporation, 306 East Baltimore Pike, 2nd Floor, Media, PA 19063

- *Family Violence & Sexual Assault Bulletin,* Family Violence & Sexual Assault Institute, 3215 Lower Ridge Road, San Diego, CA 92130

- *Feminist Periodicals: A Current Listing of Contents,* Women's Studies Librarian-at-Large, 728 State Street, 430 Memorial Library, Madison, WI 53706

- *Gay & Lesbian Abstracts,* National Information Services Corporation, 306 East Baltimore Pike, 2nd Floor, Media, PA 19063

- *IBZ International Bibliography of Periodical Literature,* Zeller Verlag GmbH & Co., P.O.B. 1949, D-49009 Osnabruck, Germany

(continued)

- *Index to Periodical Articles Related to Law,* University of Texas, 727 East 26th Street, Austin, TX 78705

- *INTERNET ACCESS (& additional networks) Bulletin Board for Libraries ("BUBL"), coverage of information resources on INTERNET, JANET, and other networks.*
  - <URL:http://bubl.ac.uk/>
  - The new locations will be found under <URL:http://bubl.ac.uk/link/>.
  - Any existing BUBL users who have problems finding information on the new service should contact the BUBL help line by sending e-mail to <bubl@bubl.ac.uk>.
  The Andersonian Library, Curran Building, 101 St. James Road, Glasgow G4 0NS, Scotland

- *Mental Health Abstracts (online through DIALOG),* IFI/Plenum Data Company, 3202 Kirkwood Highway, Wilmington, DE 19808

- *Social Work Abstracts,* National Association of Social Workers, 750 First Street NW, 8th Floor, Washington, DC 20002

- *Sociological Abstracts (SA),* Sociological Abstracts, Inc., P.O. Box 22206, San Diego, CA 92192-0206

- *Studies on Women Abstracts,* Carfax Publishing Company, P.O. Box 25, Abingdon, Oxon OX14 3UE, United Kingdom

- *Violence and Abuse Abstracts: A Review of Current Literature on Interpersonal Violence (VAA),* Sage Publications, Inc., 2455 Teller Road, Newbury Park, CA 91320

- *Women "R" CD/ROM,* Softline Information, Inc., 20 Summer Street, Stamford, CT 06901

- *Women Studies Abstracts,* Rush Publishing Company, P.O. Box 1, Rush, NY 14543

(continued)

SPECIAL BIBLIOGRAPHIC NOTES

related to special journal issues (separates)
and indexing/abstracting

❏ indexing/abstracting services in this list will also cover material in any "separate" that is co-published simultaneously with Haworth's special thematic journal issue or DocuSerial. Indexing/abstracting usually covers material at the article/chapter level.

❏ monographic co-editions are intended for either non-subscribers or libraries which intend to purchase a second copy for their circulating collections.

❏ monographic co-editions are reported to all jobbers/wholesalers/approval plans. The source journal is listed as the "series" to assist the prevention of duplicate purchasing in the same manner utilized for books-in-series.

❏ to facilitate user/access services all indexing/abstracting services are encouraged to utilize the co-indexing entry note indicated at the bottom of the first page of each article/chapter/contribution.

❏ this is intended to assist a library user of any reference tool (whether print, electronic, online, or CD-ROM) to locate the monographic version if the library has purchased this version but not a subscription to the source journal.

❏ individual articles/chapters in any Haworth publication are also available through the Haworth Document Delivery Service (HDDS).

ABOUT THE EDITOR

Rhea V. Almeida, LCSW, DVS, is Founder and Director of the Institute for Family Services in Somerset, New Jersey. She developed the Cultural Context Model, an expanded model of family therapy, and has written numerous articles on Asian Indian families, cultural perspectives in domestic violence, mentoring, unexamined assumptions of social service delivery, child development, and the intersectionality of gender, race, class, culture and sexual orientation. Editor of *Expansions of Feminist Family Theory Through Diversity* (1994, The Haworth Press, Inc.), Dr. Almeida has received an award from the American Family Therapy Academy for her work with women of color.

Transformations of Gender and Race: Family and Developmental Perspectives

CONTENTS

Foreword

It is a risky, perplexing and interesting opportunity to be invited to write the foreword to "Transformations of Gender and Race," a paradigm-shifting special issue of the *Journal of Feminist Family Therapy*. As a white feminist who has not made a significant contribution to post-colonial theory or to the clinical and political challenges of diversity, I have my doubts (as I imagine many of you do) about the appropriateness of my being positioned in this privileged place at the front of this radically unsettling volume.

Indeed, as the time to write grew near, I became increasingly uncertain as to how to proceed. When I asked Rhea Almeida, the Editor of this issue, to help me understand her thinking on the matter, she E-mailed the idea that she wanted to "include (my) voice in an expanded consciousness of feminist thought." This phrase has stayed with me because inclusiveness is a core democratic value, often betrayed, and consciousness (raising)/expansion is the promise of every liberatory movement that "brings news of (a) difference" into awareness and conversation.

So taking these terms as book-ends for my response to this richly evocative material, I have found my voice in the idea that I am here in this place not as a writer, but as a reader–a reader who can reassure other readers that this is a volume that does indeed value inclusiveness and will not shut you out, although it may well disturb and distress you along the way.

And, on the CR front, if my own experience is any guide, the cumulative effect of these essays is to move and edify, no matter how much we all thought we really did "get it" about the cruel and pernicious workings of domination and oppression. Indeed, perhaps most important to this reader is the emotional shock many of these essays deliver, as they document just how much suffering has been produced right in our midst. As we take the

[Haworth co-indexing entry note]: "Foreword." Goldner, Virginia. Co-published simultaneously in *Journal of Feminist Family Therapy* (The Haworth Press, Inc.) Vol. 10, No. 1, 1998, pp. xv-xvii; and: *Transformations of Gender and Race: Family and Developmental Perspectives* (ed: Rhea V. Almeida) The Haworth Press, Inc., 1998, pp. xi-xiii. Single or multiple copies of this article are available for a fee from The Haworth Document Delivery Service [1-800-342-9678, 9:00 a.m. - 5:00 p.m. (EST). E-mail address: getinfo@haworthpressinc.com].

measure of how "our" (white, middle-class, heterosexual) professional culture with its inevitable racism and homophobia have hurt and harmed so many of our colleagues, patients and friends, it is still hard to believe how ignorant and comfortable we have been for so long.

In the context of these intensely painful emotions, it does seem very important to me, thinking about inclusiveness, that these essays are being published in a special issue of *JFFT*. Too often in the history of radical movements, growth and change have come at the cost of factionalism, repudiation and betrayal. Perhaps this is because so much is at stake for everyone. So much has been put on the line, so much pain has been endured and inflicted, that eventually the sense of "we" begins fatefully to erode, giving way to an increasingly bitter experience of "us" and "them."

Yet the simple fact that this volume, with its weight of fact, anger and grief, much of it directed against white feminism, is published under the sign of feminism, provides living testimony that now, still, there remains a viable "we" to hold our ordeal of confronting difference. Indeed, many of the authors in this volume work with a feminist systemic construct, "differentiation through complexity," which can provide us all with a theoretical frame to help resist the impulse to break apart into smaller, simpler, weaker and more paranoid cells.

Perhaps history has made its point, and no one wants a repetition. Perhaps feminism, leavened, deepened and decentered by the sound of marginalized voices speaking in powerfully improved theoretical languages like post-colonial and queer theory, can continue to reinvent itself while growing a big tent large enough to hold us together in the process. Clearly, we all still want to talk.

And to teach and learn. This is the other important meta-message carried by this volume. These authors, despite all the injury they have endured and witnessed, want to bring not only their pain, but also their very good ideas to the table. They are suggesting, collectively, that the insights of cultural multiplicity will thicken, enrich, and ultimately transform our theories, and will, more importantly, humanize our practice in profound and essential ways. (A one-liner that distills this radical impulse goes, "as the frame is enlarged . . . the focus moves away from the search for pathology toward the search for justice" (Font, Dolan-Del Vecchio & Almeida, this volume).

These essays deliver many distilled insights like this one, as well as richly articulated analyses in which such aphorisms find their place. There is much food for thought here. Collectively, the pieces provide a superb, state of the art bibliography of contemporary thinking in cultural studies, post-colonial theory, gender theory, queer theory, as well as in clinical and research work with numerous populations that have been overlooked and undertheorized. Moreover, each essay, in one way or another, is the product of a long and deep immersion with the issues it addresses. Thus, there is a wealth of expertise and sharp observation to take to work on almost every page. There are, for example, some wonderful ideas about how to bring diversity into the lived experience of young children (Almeida, Woods & Messineo, this volume), and how to unpack the "complex linkages of diversity and adversity" that shape the lives and problems of every family we treat (Font, Dolan-Del Veccio & Almeida, this volume).

Going through this manuscript left me with the sense that these passionate and weary next-wave pioneers (both those represented in this collection, and those working and writing alongside them) have produced a collective body of work that is approaching the critical mass necessary for a paradigm shift. Just as second-wave feminism moved from a critique at the margins to a transformational theory of the whole, so diversity studies, in all its many varieties, is poised to explode our taken-for-granted categories of identity, psyche, culture and psychotherapy, and to create new theories, practices, and a brand new vision of a decentered center of gravity.

Virginia Goldner, PhD
Ackerman Institute for the Family

The Dislocation of Women's Experience in Family Therapy

Rhea V. Almeida

Can a feminist scholarship withstand the simultaneity of multiple oppressions in the context of power and privilege? Women in families experience gender, race, class, culture and sexual orientation as intersections of life.

–Rhea Almeida

FEMINISM IS . . . . "The political theory and practice to free all women–women of color, working class women, poor women, physically challenged women, lesbians, old women as well as white women, economically privileged women, heterosexual women. I myself have never been able to find out precisely what feminism is: I only know that people call me a feminist whenever I express sentiments that differentiate me from a doormat."

–Rebecca West

FEMINISM IS . . . . "If the feminist movement does not address itself to issues of race, class and imperialism, it cannot be relevant to alleviating the oppression of most of the women of the world."

–Cheryl Johnson Odim

Rhea V. Almeida, PhD, is Founder and Executive Director, Institute for Family Services, 3 Clyde Road, Suite 101, Somerset, NJ and Faculty Member, Family Institute of New Jersey, Metuchen, NJ.

[Haworth co-indexing entry note]: "The Dislocation of Women's Experience in Family Therapy." Almeida, Rhea V. Co-published simultaneously in *Journal of Feminist Family Therapy* (The Haworth Press, Inc.) Vol. 10, No. 1, 1998, pp. 1-22; and: *Transformations of Gender and Race: Family and Developmental Perspectives* (ed: Rhea V. Almeida) The Haworth Press, Inc., 1998, pp. 1-22. Single or multiple copies of this article are available for a fee from The Haworth Document Delivery Service [1-800-342-9678, 9:00 a.m. - 5:00 p.m. (EST). E-mail address: getinfo@haworthpressinc.com].

1

FEMINISM IS . . . ."A method of approaching life and politics, a way of asking questions and searching for answers, rather than a set of political conclusions about the oppression of women."

–Nancy Hartsock

FEMINISM IS . . . ."There is and must be a diversity of feminisms responsive to the different needs and concerns of different women and defined by them for themselves."

–Nilufer Catatoy Caren Grown
Aida Santiago

From *The "F" Word. A Video about Feminism*
Jarmel & Gallagher, 1994

The specifics of experience for women along a continuum of race, class and ethnicity have been submerged under one reality by dominant feminist thought: that of gender oppression. It is true that all of women's lives are connected to the patriarchal structure of society to different degrees. But not acknowledging the different dimensions of oppression limits the choices of empowerment available to women, and in some instances places them in life-threatening situations.

A social movement that is transformative must break the isomorphism of power and privilege that it critiques. Bearing witness to the invisibility/ visibility of oppression is critical to beginning a liberation process. The invisible oppression of White women and that of visibility/invisibility for women of color occur along a continuum. This universalizing of descriptors obscures critical life experiences even for White heterosexual women who fall at the margin of class privilege, while the experiences for women of color from different class strata (economically privileged, of immigrant status, lesbian, working class, disabled) are all part of a different structural and life experience that involves the simultaneity of oppression, power, and privilege (Matamala & Salazar, 1997; Narayan, 1997; Collins, 1991; Almeida, 1993; Pharr, 1988; Moraga & Anzaldua, 1983).

In this article, I bring attention to the ways in which feminism in family-therapy has contributed to the visibility of some women from diverse social and cultural locations. I also want to raise our awareness of the ways in which feminism in the field has continued to assume a position focusing solely on gender as a form of oppression. I will provide discussion about how this type of fixed or standpoint theory (Harding, 1990) excludes critical domains of women's existence, as the women in question are not necessarily White, middle-class and heterosexual. Furthermore, it raises fundamental questions about our ethics and morality with regard to feminist practice.

In preparing for this article, an analysis was planned of all the family-therapy journals to discern the percentage of articles devoted to issues of race, culture, class, and sexual orientation. However, neither *Family Process*, *Family Systems Medicine*, nor the *Journal of Marriage and Family Therapy* has taken a strong ethical stance on inclusivity. While these journals continue to be challenged about the exclusiveness of their White editorial boards, the interiorized nature of their publications and the ethics of gate-keeping, they continue to espouse in practice certain dominant notions of family theory and therapy. While they have attempted to alter their editorial leadership, they have not diversified the editorial board, nor do they require publications to be inclusive. By definition, scholarship from this "objective" view is subjective to power structures within and beyond the journal.

The birth and evolution of Journal of Feminist Family Therapy (JFFT) is another matter entirely. Its very existence is a celebrated response to the domination of editorial boards and their "gatekeeping" mandates. The JFFT has not only taken an ethical stance with regard to inclusivity, but also has the word *feminist* in its title, which stands as a notation of social and moral consciousness and a developmental landmark in family therapy. Therefore, it seems more relevant to reflect on the evolving composition of this board, as well as to provide an analysis of the journal articles with respect to gender, race, class, culture, and sexual orientation.

I provide this analysis with some uncertainty. This journal is critical to launching my visibility amid the world of publications, having published a controversial article of mine, "Sponsorship: Men Holding Men Accountable for Domestic Violence" (Almeida and Bograd, 1990)–an article that *Family Process* held for three years (1989-1990) then declined to publish. The editorial board of JFFT has moved from a membership comprised entirely of White women to a current representation of 34 White women and 11 women of color (1989-1997). After eight years of change, one-third of the editorial board are women of color. This is an overwhelming achievement in the context of editorial gatekeeping. In spite of these progressive shifts, it is necessary to invite and maintain an ongoing critique to serve as a system of accountability, central to a gender discourse that is inclusive of race, class, culture, and sexual orientation.

Included at the end of this article is an Expanded Reference Guide to Feminism for Family Therapists. The original guide was published by Judith Avis Myers in 1989.

A REVIEW OF THE ARTICLES–
JOURNAL OF FEMINIST FAMILY THERAPY (JFFT)

A total of 140 articles published from 1989 to 1997 were reviewed. Of these, 55 included dimensions of race, culture and sexual orientation. Of these 55 articles, 35 were in "special issues" dedicated to race, culture, class, and sexual orientation. Only 20 articles were inclusive of women's simultaneity of experience. When the concept of woman was described in 85 of the articles, a monolithic definition of feminine was implied: White; heterosexual; and middle-class.

Similarly, while these same feminist writings have provided a social analysis of public institutions that shape women's lives, this analysis has not provided a coherent system of intervention within the therapeutic context. Concepts of woman are most often portrayed within the interior of family life intergenerationally at its broadest construction–with references to relationships with work, child care, money, and reproductive health, with children introduced as an extension to a compartmentalized narrative. Children whose lives are exposed daily to medical hardships and dilapidated housing, while living amid life-threatening situations of street and domestic violence, are deferred to the "special-topics" publications. The mothers, sisters, and grandmothers of these children are forgotten voices in the mainstream analysis of women's lives.

This is a journal that tends to publish more material than it declines in order to counter the subjugation of voice common in the mainstream journals. Most of the articles submitted, however, represent the dominant group of feminists. When alternative authors are invited to contribute, it is usually within the context of a special topic, such as Black History Month as presented within our educational system. This particularizing of subject is conceptually and practically problematic-isomorphic to this culture's historic and circuitous mode of segregation. To illustrate, integrating the experience of African-Americans into the curriculum throughout the year is a more inclusive way to study issues of privilege for some and oppression for others, without furthering the practice of segregation.

Similarly, members on the editorial board who are people of color have participated with respect to specific areas of expertise and interest, rather than facilitating the integration of concepts of race, class, culture, and sexual orientation into all the journal writings. Editors of color have not been used to facilitate a rite of passage for those voices that might represent marginality or to shift the conceptual frameworks to include women from all groups. No system of accountability has been instituted to help monitor some of the silencing that is a natural evolution of those with access to various forms of power and privilege (albeit different from that granted to White men).

ECONOMICS OF WOMEN OF COLOR

What are the distinctions between women who have achieved pay parity of 60 to 70 cents on the dollar with benefits and those who still struggle at 30 cents to the dollar with no benefit package? (Emerge, 1997). The following statistics reveal a distinctively different profile for White women versus their counterparts of color.

1. With regards to the prison systems, in the past decade, the female prison population has grown by 202 percent, the male by 112 percent, 73 percent of women in prison are under 30 years of age and 58 percent of women in prison are women of color and the number of black women in federal or state prison or a local jail rose nearly 200 percent from 1985-1995 (Bureau of Justice Statistics; National Coalition for Jail Reform, Washington, D.C.).
2. The imprisonment of women has left an estimated 167,000 children without mothers.
3. Two of every 5 African-American women over 65 live in poverty (Ries & Stone, 1992).
4. Prostitution–40 percent of street prostitutes are women of color; 55 percent of those arrested are women of color; 85 percent of prostitutes sentenced to do jail time are women of color (Sex, Work, Writings by Women in the Sex Industry, 1987).
5. By the year 2005, women's participation in the labor force will have risen by 26 percent. Latino women, Asian women, Native Americans, Alaskan natives, and Pacific Islanders will have the fastest growth–80 percent; African-American women's labor force growth will be 34 percent (U.S. Department of Labor Women's Bureau, 1992).
6. In a 1982 survey, 92.5 percent of female-owned businesses were owned by white women, 3.8 percent by African-American women, 2.1 percent by Latina women, and 1.6 percent by Asian women (U.S. Department of Labor Women's Bureau, 1992).
7. With regards to disabilities, 13.8 percent of African-American women have work disabilities, compared with 7.7 percent of white women (U.S. Department of Labor Women's Bureau, 1992).
8. The maternal mortality rate for whites is 5.9 deaths per thousand; for African Americans it is 19.5 per thousand (Statistical Abstracts of the United States, 1991).

9. While African-American women comprise 19 percent of the single women in this country, 59 percent of all single mothers are African Americans (U.S. Department of Labor Women's Bureau, 1991). Of the 4.6 million Hispanic families in the U.S. in 1988, 1 million were headed by women (U.S. Department of Labor Women's Bureau, 1991).
10. While 57 percent of all children in female-headed households live below the poverty level, 79 percent of African-American children in female-headed households live below the poverty level (The American Woman, 1990).

Contrasting these statistics with those presented in the journal would elicit a different kind of theorizing. Instead, dilemmas are presented in the context of middle-class White women struggling to balance work and family, struggling with their partners over whether they can hire extra help, while the profile of the "help" and her problems never makes it to the page. While the "second shift" has received central attention, the "third shift"–that is, taking care of one's own home after servicing the communities of White families, a familiar construct in the lives of women of color–has yet to be defined conceptually and clinically. I introduce the concept of "third shift" to describe the transition for women of color from predominantly domestic work to various institutional jobs in hospital laundries, institutional kitchens, paper mills of corporations, lower-paid staff in day-care facilities, and as cleaners of public institutions. These jobs usually entail long hours, low wages, hazardous working conditions, and no medical benefits. These women rarely can afford childcare of any kind (The Facts About Women, 1993).

The writings of Crenshaw (1994) and Minerbrook (1993) further elucidate this point. They describe the redlining by real-estate corporations that have contributed to the accumulation of wealth within White middle-class families and the stagnation and povertization of middle-class communities of color. This is accomplished through the sustained increase in value of housing and school districts in White neighborhoods, and the sustained devaluing of homes and schools in communities of color. While White families starting out have twice the income of their counterparts of color, they own 10 times the wealth (U.S. Census, 1988). Home equity accounts for more than 40 percent of this difference.

Clinical inquiry regarding money in terms of job loss or access, money in terms of education and housing, or support for the prison industry is not translated into questions of moral reasoning for these women and their families, thus resulting in a morality that privileges certain families over others. How can the families of these women heal if such critical information is obscured in favor of discussing psychological processes within their relationships without examining the social/cultural context? Or if they are forced to adapt to White middle-class ideas of oppression and adaptation? How can this issue be addressed ethically if money is only spoken of as a construction by the couple or, in the case of a single mother or other family unit, in the way of salaries, management of investments or inheritances, within the interior of their relationships?

First-generation immigrant women experience added strains. The process of adaptation is somewhat easier for white immigrant women from European countries, who are romanticized in spite of their accents, rather than marginalized like many immigrant women of color. The "third shift" for many established immigrant women is born of continuous efforts to protect financial earnings, since inheritance is not a reasonable expectation in their lifetime; the struggle of coping with fewer members in an extended family; the paradoxical reliance on this system that does not tend to support women in work; and the continuous stress of re-creating connections of community support, lost in the transition from their "homeland" (Almeida, 1996; Garcia-Preto, 1996; Baca Zinn, 1994-5; Crenshaw, 1994).

A hidden assumption in dominant feminist discourse accords women of color and immigrant women the same power, privilege, and "cushion" of support as White women with similar levels of education. While many White women may experience similar struggles in their efforts to create and maintain connections for their children, the level of anxiety and health implications for immigrant women are often far greater. In addition to these basic structural tasks, these immigrant women also have all of the same basic responsibilities as their White counterparts in home, family, and community life.

STATISTICS REGARDING MEN OF COLOR

A feminist scholarship that is inclusive must also consider men's lives. The experience of oppression for many women of color is linked not only to gender but to race in their connection to white women. While White women as culture bearers of the patriarchy may critique their fathers and male partners, they are usually protective of their sons, nephews and brothers, therefore participating indirectly in the curtailing of resources and institutional oppression of both men and women of color. Knowledge about the men in the lives of women of color is essential to deconstructing and understanding the choices these women make. A scholarship that is focused on solidarity amongst diverse women must at the very least acknowledge the scholarship of men's lives across various social locations.

An example of inclusivity would be the analysis of incarceration of a disproportionate number of men of color in this country and the emotional and political impact on the lives of women of color? Here are some facts to consider:

1. From 1985 to 1995 the number of African-American men in federal, state and local prisons rose 130 percent compared to 90 percent for Whites. African-American males constitute approximately 46 percent of all U.S. prisoners. The prison industry currently generates $30-$40 billion annually and is growing.
2. Wall Street supports the expansion of the prison system through corporate structuring for the prison system (Emerge, 1997).

PARENTING IN THE CONTEXT OF RACE

When addressing the problems and needs of children in the literature, White middle-class children are most often the focus. For example, the stresses of parenting for women in general, given the second-shift analysis, is a feminist issue. Given the dimensions of the "third shift," parenting for women of color is further constrained within the intersection of gender, race, class, culture and sexual orientation–the experience of "institutional entrapment." I use the phrase "institutional entrapment" to describe the multiple ways in which institutions limit access to minimal standards of well-being and legitimize varied forms of abuse towards women of color and their families. For example, competing sources of funding and mission statements shaped by a population's single presenting problem (e.g., from mental health, health and illness to battered women, women with addictions) fracture the lives of women and children on the margin (Almeida et al., 1998–in press).

A discussion of parenting that factors in dimensions of class would consider differences in intervention within the context of affluence versus poverty (Gavazzi, Alford, & McKenry, 1996; Lantz & Alford, 1995). Therefore, not all techniques of reinforcement and discipline structure would be helpful to parents. Adding the dimensions of race further raises the necessity to expand our clinical descriptions of parenting. Denby and Alford (1996) contend that discipline styles unique to low-socioeconomic women/mothers of color do exist. However, these are often compared to White middle-class women/mothers as the standard. In researching a group of heterogeneous families of African-American origin, these authors found that some of the primary aims of discipline were related to issues of racial socialization. Goals for teaching their children about racial situations they might encounter included the following (Denby and Alford, 1996):

1. Keeping children out of situations where society would hold them responsible (e.g., blame them for events not in their field of responsibility) [The notation in parentheses this author's];
2. Maneuvering into any segment of society [without being] viewed as a threat;
3. Teaching children that they must work hard to counter the discrimination prevalent in society;
4. Teaching survival techniques as they relate to race differences.

These parents described their parenting styles as "stern" compared to their White counterparts, which they described as "relaxed." These differences in parenting styles are another reflection of the experiences that White parents versus parents of color experience vis-à-vis our cultural institutions.

Lastly, the dominant discourse on feminism has attended to the limitations of traditional development theory (Erikson, 1950, 1968; Kohlberg, 1981; Freud, 1905) as it informs the lives of women. Much of the literature in the journal has focused on the relational theories of Gilligan (1988) and her colleagues. Although this relational scholarship has informed us about the differences in moral domains between the genders it leaves out translations of power. It is critical that our therapeutic theorizing and systems of intervention–with girls, children of color, gay and lesbian youth–include the feminist critique, and that this critique be inclusive (Almeida et al., 1998–in press).

DOMINANT FEMINISM IN THE DOMESTIC VIOLENCE MOVEMENT– A CASE STUDY

It is also useful to consider the shelter movement, which represents a strong social movement in support of women's rights. This system has obtained rights for battered women with respect to judicial equity, transitional living, job training, and child care standards, as well as specific standards for batterers' intervention services. This latter gain is critical in attempting to dismantle institutionalized forms of masculinity. The lack of protection provided to battered women of color by the courts and shelter movement is glaring, however–the White feminist movement has failed to provide a range of options for women from diverse social locations (Bograd, 1996; Hart, 1997; Crenshaw, 1994; Narayan, 1995).

Writings by Beth Richie (1985) reflect the large statistic of African-American battered women as prisoners on Rykers Island for killing their partners, a desperate response by women to a society whose institutions have not protected them over the years.

Yet the most significant gap in the experience of service delivery for women of color was that of the shelters, its advocacy on their behalf, and the judicial and law-enforcement systems (Narayan, 1997; Crenshaw, 1994). During this period, White battered women were protected by the shelter movement, their economic situation improved markedly, and those who murdered their partners received access to legal defenses that argued the role of retaliatory violence within the context of domestic violence. At the same time, women of color were not only indicted, but also convicted as felons for their crimes of domestic violence. Women of color, African-American women in particular, are currently being arrested for such misdemeanors as stealing bread from grocery stores to feed their children.

THE PERSONAL NARRATIVE AS A FEMINIST FORM

White women as family therapists have direct access and privilege to all that develops from these societally sanctioned constructions of womanhood. These constructions of woman leave intact and unanalyzed the privileges of White women, along with the powerful roles of culture bearers and resource handlers that they hold globally. White women as family therapists and "feminists" claim the name and language that stands for equity among all human beings, and for raising the standard of life for all women. Launching a journal that has embraced the writings of authors otherwise excluded in the dominant journals has added a sense of integrity, but breeds complacency at the same time. What is evolving as scholarship is a dangerous brand of self-focus and a deep penchant for privileging of self/personal stories.

This shift structures a politic that is insufficiently inclusive. Such feminist strategies that privilege privatized gender fail to build coalitions among diverse groups of women. Women who locate their struggle within the intersection of racism, colonialism, imperialism, and capitalism define their politics in a *collective* (Mohanty, Russo, & Torres, 1991). Obscuring the collective in favor of the personal/private masks the specificity of constraints and impedes possibilities for therapeutic solutions (Hawkesworth, 1997).

What would it take to write about welfare and the distinctions of public institutional life that erode the identity of millions of women who are "other?" Writing about these experiences is not always poetic. However, marking these structural distinctions serves to voice the experiences of all women in their varied forms of oppression, within varying contexts of power and privilege.

How does a personal narrative deconstruct the horror of an undocumented Vietnamese woman, Meiki, who has no legal immigration status in the paper production section of a corporation? An alien living in a homeless shelter, covering her body in the 102° F heat wave because she is afraid the mice will chew on her bleeding toes. She is battered but cannot go to a domestic violence shelter for women because she has a 14-year-old! (Shelters generally do not house women with adolescent male children.) These are women who speak another language, women who, because of cultural, racial, and economic restraints, are not certain if leaving their partners is the most viable solution for them. What are the solutions of a collective feminism?

Women who require support from public institutions such as jobs, housing, safe schools for their children and police protection are the women who are made invisible because of the scholarship that for 20 years has focused on the dominant, common solutions. What are the solutions of a collective feminism?

Is there a difference between personal anthologies and the benchmark of "the personal is political"? Perhaps for White women who have achieved some equity in their world, these structures of inequity hold less meaning. When they do hold meaning, the power of describing it within the structure of a self-portrait has great appeal. Continuing to articulate the power differentials in a time of "organized backlash" places hard earned gains at risk, making complacency a natural response.

What about the political is personal–the benchmark for women of color? Is it accidental, deliberate, or just another face of domination that such critical conceptions of gender have eluded the analysis, writings and application of an entire group of White feminists? I have overheard a number of well-respected "feminists" at various conferences expressing concern over the emphasis on cultural diversity, fearing that it will dilute conversations about gender. Does this mean that women in these "other" cultural domains have concerns that cannot be framed within a Western feminist analysis, or is it that women who are "other" matter less in the formal scholarship?

Within our own cultural circles, Third World Feminists have had to contend with being subjugated to male voices in the name of combating "outside" forces such as colonialism, racism, and anti-Islamic forces all for the good of a solid national or ethnic/cultural identity (Narayan, 1997; Almeida, 1997). As Cherrie Moraga (1994) states:

> Over and over again, Chicanas trivialize the women's movement as being merely a white middle-class thing, having little to offer women of color. . . . Interestingly, it is perfectly acceptable among Chicano males to use white theoreticians, e.g., Marx and Engels, to develop a theory of Chicano oppression. It is unacceptable, however, for the Chicana to use white sources by women to develop a theory of Chicana oppression. (p. 38)

In a paper presented in *JFFT* (Almeida, 1993), I offered a feminist analysis that was inclusive of women in their diversity. While the restructuring of invisibility has been a key factor in the analysis and distribution of resources for White women, visibility/invisibility assumes a different subordinate form for women of color, and an attendant lack of resources is a key issue. Some examples of gains that White women have more claim to are accumulations of resources, closing of the gap in pay parity, access to higher learning in increasing proportions, pregnancy benefits and leave, legalized abortion, entrance into male academies and the military, and sexual harassment in the workplace legislation. All of these freedoms earned are through a strategizing of the *collective*.

RACE AS A SOCIAL CONSTRUCT IN THE EVOLUTION OF POWER

While the writings about women within family structures has developed out of a scholarship that attends to the ways in which institutions maintain the power and privilege of the patriarchy, this scholarship has not been applied to the social construction of race. Race, like gender, is a social construct that historically has assigned power differentials according to skin color and biological characteristics. Christensen (1997) describes the fluid boundaries evidenced in the racial categorizations of White individuals, with Ashkenazi Jews and other light-skinned ethnics being offered access into the economic and labor markets in this country. The collective of economic and political power by European and American forces was derived from a shared and legitimized process of slavery and colonial expansion. This concentration of economic and political power continues today, albeit in better organized systems of delivery. This misappropriation occurs through the organized control of job opportunities, housing markets, medical benefits, political power, and general control of market resources. This creates life-threatening situations for women of color and their children, in ways that further separate them from White middle-class women.

I think that the launching of personal narratives in the context of this evolving success from invisibility to visibility reifies the oppressed as woman–White woman. This is the meaning of "standpoint" theory. In an essay entitled "With Whom Do You Believe Your Lot Is Cast?: White Feminism and Racism," Christensen (1997) relates this to the heavy reliance on "personalized knowledge" or "consciousness raising," by the second wave of the American feminist movement. This belief is not unlike that of Paulo Freire (1972), which rests on the assumption that a "communally derived interpretation of the experiences of oppressed people provides fertile ground for the development of theories of their oppression and liberation."

The use of these general experiences by women of color to generate theories are radically different from such theories by White women. The universalizing of women's experiences that results from this process legitimizes a segregation from the lives of women of color, lesbians/bisexuals, working-class women, and others. Furthermore, the extension of this type of analysis to explore White women's relationship to racism is seriously flawed. White women in this context are not entirely the oppressed, but participants in the oppression of "others."

So when a story of a mother and child is told with respect to illness, their shared experience focuses heavily on the oppression of their lives by the institutions that *support* them; what is silenced is the shared experience of a woman and her child in the inner city who not only face the catastrophe of illness but also that of institutional exclusion–and often institutional decimation. Such exclusion and decimation is often carried out by White women as culture bearers and caretakers of the White-male establishment. Offices of the welfare and labor departments, schools as well as real-estate agents, are only some examples of how White women are used as culture bearers and caretakers–participating as oppressors of women and men who are "other."

The deconstruction of wealth and power along the dimensions of gender, race, class, and sexual orientation within all of our institutions is critical to an analysis of feminism that is inclusive of all women.

TRAINING IN FEMINIST FAMILY THERAPY

Supervision and training are the critical underpinnings for advancing the scholarship of feminist practice. Over the past eight years, a number of articles have been written on integrating feminism into the curriculum and supervision. The content has varied from infusing the training with feminist readings to an analysis of structure and process that is female-centered. Yet as feminist teachers/writers critique the context from which they teach, they describe a continued perpetuation of hierarchical systems by male colleagues in the family therapy field as well as an absence of conversation surrounding the politics of race, culture and sexual orientation within these training contexts.

To illustrate, an article by Elizabeth Sirles (1994) was excellent in terms of its complete inclusion of structure and process as it related to numerous White feminists' readings; however, the inclusion of race, culture, class, and sexual orientation was minimal. Similarly, the issue on "Reflections on Feminist Family Therapy Training" (1997) perpetuated the standpoint (Harding, 1990) theory with two White women as editors. It is useful to ask what differences might have emerged around structure and content of the issue had one of the editors been of color? For example, the opening article described a white feminist's experience of trying to include feminist ideals within the curriculum and supervision context of a white, male-run training institute. It might be noteworthy to ponder about the co-creation of theory had a feminist of color been one of the co-editors; or a lesbian? a lesbian of color? How might her voice have contributed to the experiences of shared feminism within a similar context? Or a different context? Articles contained in this same issue included one by a Latina student who by her own description is powerless to shift the structure of training; the other article that attended to diversity also focused on curriculum without a critique of the hidden dimensions of academia. A critical analyses of the context from where the teaching is launched is as relevant as the curriculum itself. Obscuring this analysis continues the legacy of absence in the discourse of women.

CONCLUSION–
CASE EXAMPLE–
INTEGRATING THE SIMULTANEITY
OF A DIVERSE WOMAN'S EXPERIENCE

A white corporate executive is married to a dark-skinned Latino professional woman, both are in their early forties. They have three children–two daughters and a son–ages 12, 9, and 5. The presenting problem is "mid-life dilemmas of a couple's experience." He has a relatively successful career that she supported through their 14 years of marriage. Her career, in which she has *invested* more recently has taken off. He complains about her preoccupation with her work and his wish to relocate on behalf of the "family's" possibilities for upward mobility. He complains about her not being interested in him as much as her career. However, there are no signs of neglect of their children expressed either by them or outside systems. He complains about *Her* anger and she, about *His* emotional and second/third-shift unavailability.

A common approach to gathering more information and reformulating the problem/solution context might be as follows:

1. Elicit their story of connection to one another and to larger systems.
2. Track legacies of loss.
3. Elicit information regarding the second-shift/third-shift responsibilities.
4. Explore the couple's relationships with their respective families of origin with discussion of their ethnic/cultural differences.
5. Define the life-cycle stage of this family, as well as that of their respective families.

This line of inquiry continues to neutralize the institution of "couple-hood." While certainly a far cry from the position of reciprocity and mutuality, it continues to privilege the couple–a legitimized unit of western patriarchy.

Inquiry ought to be along lines of *accountability*:

1. Elicit the shaping origins of his masculinity within his family and public institutions that socialize and maintain his "normalcy" through life–schools, peers, recreation, camps, college, and work experiences. What are the centers of ongoing support for his experience of masculinity? Explore rigidities embedded within heterosexism and homophobia; create a context that embodies conversation regarding sexual orientation.
2. Elicit his views on women: their roles, familiarity with their traditional norms of socialization in the family, at work and in the larger culture, as they relate to his description of masculinity.
3. Explore his development as a sexual being: rites of passage along a continuum from seduction of women to pornography and S/M clubs: An alarmingly large number of boys, beginning at age nine, and men of all ages are consuming pornography "on-line" and vis-

iting sex clubs, choices we know are assaultive to women. These rites of passage play a crucial role in destroying the very fabric of intimate connections. Attempts to deconstruct exploitation by men of affluence toward all women with particular distinctions toward women of color, is thus introduced–a different dimension of moral inquiry.

4. Explore his relationship with work: given that this relationship is the most critical aspect of a man's expression of masculinity, it is the more relevant system for intervention. This is the "couple" that both obscures and overshadows the more familiar couple system. Discuss his connections to other men in senior positions, his ability to work collaboratively at work (note: with the advancement of legislation regarding workplace harassment, it is crucial to elicit a man's views and responses as they impact relationships with his female peers, subordinates and his intimate partner). With men who are unemployed men or have limited access to work this heightening of masculinity within the interior of the familial relationship is of particular relevance with differences attributable to the intersectionality of race, class, culture and sexual orientation. These responses will provide a richness of information regarding his views and expectations within family life. These questions assist in the location of his emotional complaints which quite possibly might arise from diminished experiences of manhood originating within the overarching context of male influence–work. Consequently, the expressions of depression around loss of status and achievement around work are channeled into intimate life. His demands for relational response and his expressions of emotional dissatisfaction are legitimized within the system of "coupling" and familial life. What about the possibility that his ambivalence around emotional caretaking, familial responsibility and commitment are related to rigid roles of masculinity and/or denial of sexual orientation?

Inquiry directed toward his partner should be along lines of *empowerment*:

1. What are her links of support within her family, his family, the community, and work? What kind of support do each of these systems offer her? What are the barriers she faces as a Latina? As an African-Caribbean woman with a pronounced accent? What are the ways in which her professional role acts as a buffering system? How are her children both supported and marginalized? How does she have to *expand* herself to accommodate these societal responses?

2. Express curiosity about her vigor to survive and conversations of validation for her location within a complex and burdened web of life–that of gender, race, class, culture and sexual orientation. Track all of the ways in which her role as a woman is prescribed and maintained?

3. Instead of focusing on her anger (defined by her husband)–which serves as armor to keep her out of psychiatric institutions as well as maintain her clarity in multiple contexts–it might be relevant to elicit all of the detailed ways in which she orchestrates the second and third shifts for her family, her work, and in the community. The very quantification of this process is tremendously empowering to all women and to women of color in particular.

4. Discuss legacies of loss within the family, around country of origin and connections there, through illness, and continuously through the intersectionality of gender, race, culture and sexual orientation.

5. Follow the more conventional line of inquiry regarding her own childhood, her family's expectations of her in marriage, childrearing, and occupation.

This case analysis suggests some ways to address the simultaneity of dislocation in the lives of diverse women. Evident are the possible dimensions of dislocation inspite of this woman's class privilege. The case also underscores the necessity of not intervening in the "same" way with both genders. It is a moral and ethical imperative that feminists as change agents use their power to reconstruct the paradigm of intervention to include those systems with greater power (Bograd, 1991). Privileging the intrapsychic and nuclear family systems over other contexts of relationship is to collude with systems of domination. Locating the very description of problem and solution within the *interior* of a couple's/family's life, with occasional reference to second shift responsibilities, money, or work will not transform the lives of men. The transformation of men's lives is critical to the lives of millions of women.

REFERENCES

Almeida, R. (1996). *Asian Indian families: Hindu Christian/Muslim*. In McGoldrick, M., Giordano, J., & Pierce, J.K. (Eds). Ethnicity & Family Therapy, Second Edition. New York: Guilford Press.

Almeida, R. (1997). *Has the Focus on Multiculturalism Resulted in Inadequate Attention to Factors Such as Gender, Social Class, and Sexual Orientation?* In de Anda, D. (Ed.). Controversial Issues in Multiculturalism.

Almeida, R. (1993). *Unexamined assumptions and service delivery systems: Feminist theory and racial exclusions.* Journal of Feminist Family Therapy Vol. 2 (3/4), pp. 234-256.

Almeida, R. (1998). *The Cultural Context Model. Revisioning Family Therapy: Race, Culture, Gender in Clinical Practice.* McGoldrick M., Giordano, J. & Pierce, J.K. (Eds.). Ethnicity & Family Therapy, Second Edition. New York: Guilford Press.

Almeida, R., Bograd, M. (1990). *Sponsorship: Men holding men accountable for domestic violence.* Journal of Feminist Family Therapist, Vol. 2 (3/4).

Almeida, R., Messineo, T., & Woods, R. (1998). The Intesectionality of Child Development: Race, Gender, Class, Culture and Sexual Orientation. In Press.

Baca Zinn, M. (1994-5). *New Questions, New Answers: Rethinking Social Science Theories and Latino Families.* In Family Resource Coalition Report, No. 3 & 4.

Bograd, M. (1996). Culture Conference Keynote Address. Family Institute of NJ.

Collins, P. (1991). *Black Feminist Thought: knowledge, consciousness, and the politics of empowerment.* New York: Routledge.

Crenshaw, K.W. (1994). *Mapping the Margins: Intersectionality, Identity, Politics and Violence Against Women of Color.* In Fineman, M.A. & Mykituik, R. (Eds.). The Public Nature of Private Violence. New York: Routledge.

Christensen, K. (1997). *"With Whom Do You Believe your Lot is Cast?" White Feminists and Racism.* In SIGNS: Journal of Women in Culture and Society, vol. 22, no. 3. The University of Chicago.

Denby, R. & Alford, K. (1996). *Understanding African American Discipline Styles: Suggestions for Effective Social Work Intervention.* Journal of Multicultural Social Work Vol. 4(3). The Haworth Press, Inc.

Emerge. (1997). October Issue.

Erikson, E.H. (1950). *Identity and life cycle: Selected Papers.* Psychological Issues (Monograph).

Freire, P. (1972). *Pedagogy of the Oppressed.* New York: Herder & Herder.

Freud, S. (1905). *Three essays on the theory of sexuality, VII.* In The Standard Edition of the Complete Psychological Works of Sigmund Freud (1953-1974). London: Hogarth Press.

Garcia-Preto, N. (1997). *Bridging two worlds: Latinas in the USA.* In McGoldrick M., Giordano, & Pierce, J.K. (Eds.). Ethnicity & Family Therapy, Second Edition. New York: Guilford Press.

Gavazzi, S., Alford, K., & Mckenry, P. *Culturally Specific Programs For Foster Care Youth: The Sample Case of an African Rites of Passage Program.* Family Relation April 1996.

Gilligan, C., Ward, J.V., Taylor, J., & Bardige, B. (1988). *Mapping the moral domain.* Massachusetts: Harvard Press.

Harding, S. (1990). *Feminism, Science, and the Anti-Enlightenment Critiques.* In Nicholson 1990-83-106.

Hart, B. (1997). Bridging the Gap–Cross-Cultural Perspectives on Batterers Interventions–Pennsylvania Coalition for Domestic Violence.

Hawkesworth, M. (1997). *Confounding Gender.* In Signs: Journal of Women in Culture and Society, vol. 22, no. 3. 649-682. The University of Chicago, Ill.

Jarmel, M. & Gallagher, E. (1995). *The "F" Word.* Women Make Movies, New York, New York.

Kohlberg, L. (1981). *The philosophy of moral development: Moral stages and the idea of justice: Essays on moral development, 1.* San Francisco, California: Harper & Row.

Lantz, J. & Alford, K. (1995). *Existential Family Treatment with an Urban-Appalachian Adolescent.* Journal of Family Psychotherapy Vol. 6(4). The Haworth Press, Inc.

Matamala, M.I. & Salazar (1997). *Adolescence and Motherhood.* Instantes, Vol. 6(1).

Minerbrook, S. (1993). *Home Ownership Anchors the Middle Class, but Lending Games Sink Many Prospective Owners.* Emerge: Black America's Newsmagazine, October, 42-48.

Mohanty, C., Russo, A., & Torres, L. (1991). *Third World Women and the Politics of Feminism.* Bloomington: Indiana University Press.

Moraga, C. & Anzaldua, G. (1983). *This bridge called my back.* Kitchen Table. New York: Women of Color Press.

Moraga, C. (1994). *From a Long Line of Vendidas: Chicanos and Feminism.* Theorizing Feminism: Parallel Trends in the Humanities and Social Sciences. Colorado: Westview Press.

Narayan, U. (1997). *Dislocating cultures: Identities, Traditions, and Third World Feminism.* Routledge, N.Y.

Narayan, U. (1995). *Male-Order Brides: Immigrant Women, Domestic Violence and Immigration Law.* Hypatia 10, 1.

National Coalition for Jail Reform, Washington, D.C.

New York Times (November 30, 1992). *Prisons Challenged by Women Behind Bars.*

Richie, B. (1985). *Battered Black Women: A Challenge for the Black Community.* The Black Scholar. March/April.

Ries, P. & Stone, A.J. (1992). The American Woman, 1992-93 (Eds.). New York: W.W. Norton.

Pharr, S. (1988). *Homophobia: A weapon of sexism.* Arkansas: Chardon Press.

Rex, S.E. (1990). The American Woman, 1990-1991 (Eds.). New York: W.W. Norton.

Sirles, E.A. (1994). *Teaching Feminist Family Therapy: Practicing What We Preach.* Journal of Feminist Family Therapy, Vol. 6(1). The Haworth Press, Inc.

Sex, Work, Writings by Women in the Sex Industry. (1987). Cleiss Press.

The American Woman. (1992-93). New York, W.W. Norton.

The American Woman. (1990-91). New York, W.W. Norton.

The Facts About Women. (1993). New York: The New Press.

EXPANDED REFERENCE GUIDE TO FEMINISM
FOR FAMILY THERAPISTS

Almeida, R., Woods, R., Messineo, T., & Font, R. (1996). *The Cultural Context Model: A Socioeducational Approach to Family Therapy.* In McGoldrick M. (Ed.), Re-visioning Family Therapy: Culture, Race, and Gender. New York: Guilford Press.

Almeida, R., Wood, R., Messineo, T., Font, R., & Heer, C. (1994). *Violence in the Lives of the Racially and Sexually Different: A public and private dilemma.* Journal of Feminist Family Therapy, Vol. 5 (3/4).

Anzaldua, G. (1990). *Making Face, Making Soul.* San Francisco: Aunt Lute Books.

Brooks, G. (1995). *Nine Parts of Desire: Hidden World of Islamic Women.* New York: Bantam Doubleday publishing.

Chakravorty, G.S. (1990). *The Post-Colonial Critic: Interviews, Strategies, Dialogues.* New York: Routledge.

Comas-Diaz, L. & Greene, B. (1994). *Women of Color–Integrating Ethnic and Gender Identities in Psychotherapy.* New York: Guilford Press.

Collins, P. (1990). *Black Feminist Thought: knowledge, consciousness and the politics of empowerment.* New York: Routledge.

Crenshaw, K. (1993). *Race, Gender, and Violence Against Women: Convergences, Divergences and Other Black Feminist Conundrums.* In Marion, M. (Ed.), Family Matters: Readings on Family Lives and the Law. New York: New Press.

Crenshaw, K.W. (1994). *Mapping the Margins: Intersectionality, Identity Politics, and Violence Against Women of Color.* In Fineman, M.A. & Mykitiuk, R. (Eds.), The Public Nature of Private Violence. New York: Routledge.

Crow Dog, M. & Erdoes, R. (1990). *Lakota Woman.* New York: HarperCollins Publishers.

Dasen, P. (1977). *Piagetian psychology: Cross-cultural contributions.* New York: Gardner Press.

Dimmitt, C. (1993). *Women as Mothers: Historical and Cultural Contexts in the United States from 1700-1900.* Journal of Feminist Family Therapy Vol. 5, No. 1, pp. 67-80.

Dobash, R.E. & Dobash, R.P. (1992). Chapters 7 & 8. *Women, Violence & Social Change.* London: Routledge Press.

Eisler, R. (1987). *The Chalice and the Blade: Our History Our Future.* New York: Harper & Row.

Gunn-Allen, P. (1976). *The relative importance of social class and ethnicity.* In Human Development Vol. 19, pp. 56-64.

Havighurst R. (1976). *The relative importance of social class and ethnicity in Human Development* Vol. 19, pp. 56-64.

Hayslip, Le, Ly, & Wurts, J. (1989). *A Vietnamese Woman's Journey from War to Peace–When Heaven and Earth Changed Places.* New York: Penguin Books.

Herron, A. (1994). *Two Teenagers in Twenty: Writings by gay and lesbian youth.* Boston: Alyson Publications.

hooks, b. (1984). *Feminist Theory: From Margin to Center.* Boston: South End Press.

hooks, b. (1990). *Yearning: Race, Gender, and Cultural Politics.* Boston: South End Press.

hooks, b. & West, C. (1991). *Breaking Bread: Insurgent Black Intellectual Life.* Boston: South End Press.

hooks, b. (1996). *Reel to Real: race, sex and class at the movies.* New York: Routledge.

Lorde, A. (1984). *Sister Outsider.* CA: Crossing Press.

Maccoby, E.E. (1990). *Gender and relationships: A developmental account.* American Psychologist Vol. 45, pp. 513-520.

Mcintosh, P. (1988). *White Privilege and Male Privilege: A Personal Account of Coming to See Correspondences Through Work in Women's Studies.* Working Paper No. 89. Massachusetts: Wellesley College Center for Research on Women.

Mernissi, F. (1994). *Dreams of Trespass: Tales of Harem Girlhood.* New York: Addison-Wesley.

Minh-Ha, T. (1991). *When the Moon Waxes Red: Representation, Gender and Cultural Politics.* New York: Routledge.

Pearsall, M. (1997). *The other within us: Feminist Explorations of women and aging.* Colorado: Westview Press.

Perry, D. (1993). *Back Talk: Women Writers Speak Out.* New Brunswick: Rutgers.

Pipher, M. (1994). *Reviving Ophelia.* New York: Ballantine Books.

Rajan, R.S. (1993). *Real & Imagined Women: gender, culture and postcolonialism.* New York: Routledge.

Rich, A. (1986). *Of Woman Born: Motherhood Experience and Institution.* New York: W.W. Norton.

Smith, B. (1994). *Interracial Books for Children . . .* BULLETIN Vol. 14, No. 3 & 4, pp. 7-8.

Smith, B. (1983). *Home Girls–A Black Feminist Anthology.* New York. Kitchen Table: Women of Color Press.

Sok-Kyong, K., Chi-won, K., & Chong-hui, O. (1989). *Words of Farewell: Stories by Korean Women Writers.* Washington: Seal Press.

Walker, A. & Parmar, P. (1993). *Warrior Marks: Female Genital Mutilation and the Sexual Blinding of Women.* New York: Harcourt Brace & Company.

Wallace, M. (1990). *Black Macho and the Myth of the Superwoman.* New York: Verso.

FILMS OF LIBERATION

All of the films listed below can be obtained from:

Women Make Movies, Inc.
462 Broadway, Suite 500 D
New York, N.Y. 10013

Telephone: 1-212-925-0606
Fax: 1-212-925-2052

These films provide stories of liberation for women from diverse social locations. Their commonality is a passion for personal justice and social empowerment.

Jarmel, M. & Gallagher, E. (1994). *The "F" Word. A Video about Feminism.*
Rosenwasser, P. & Rudman, L. (1992). *Visionary Voices–Women on Power.*
Gee, D. (1988). *Slaying the Dragon.*
Rogers, G. (1994). *The Vienna Tribunal.*
Milwe, B. (1990). *Women: The New Poor.*
Light, A. (1993). *Dialogues with Madwomen.*
High, K. (1989). *I Need Your Full Cooperation.*
Women with Physical Disabilities (1982). *The Disabled Women's Theatre Project.*
Sanchez-Padilla, B. (1993). *De Mujer a Mujer (From Woman to Woman).*
Colbert, L. & Cardona, D. (1992). *Thank God I'm a Lesbian.*
Parmar, P. (1991). *Kush.*
Parmar, P. (1988). *Sari Red.*
Negron-Muntaner, F. (1994). *Brincando El Charco: Portrait of a Puerto Rican.*

Child Development: Intersectionality of Race, Gender, Class, and Culture

Rhea V. Almeida
Rosemary Woods
Theresa Messineo

SUMMARY. This paper presents a theory of child development which integrates race, class, gender and culture as central factors that structure this development in fundamental ways. Human development evolves within the context of our social roles, which are fundamentally organized and bounded by our position within the class, gender, racial and cultural structure of society. This theory can be used to assess a child's maturity and to guide clinical intervention. Traditional theories of child development have overfocused on discrete tasks and stages in the evolution of a self-defined primarily by a child's level of achievement and autonomy. By contrast, our theory defines maturity by our ability to live in respectful relation to others and to our complex and multifaceted world (Almeida, Woods, Messineo, & Font, 1998). Maturity in this conceptualization requires the ability to communicate (trust), collaborate (interdependence), re-

Rhea V. Almeida, PhD, is Founder and Executive Director, Institute for Family Services, 3 Clyde Road, Suite 101, Somerset, NJ 08873, and Faculty Member, Family Institute of New Jersey, Metuchen, NJ. Rosemary Woods, MSW, is Assistant Director, Institute for Family Services, Somerset, NJ, and Family Therapist, South Brunswick Schools, Monmouth Junctions, NJ. Theresa Messineo, MSW, is Co-Director, Institute for Family Services, Somerset, NJ.

[Haworth co-indexing entry note]: "Child Development: Intersectionality of Race, Gender, Class, and Culture." Almeida, Rhea V., Rosemary Woods, and Theresa Messineo. Co-published simultaneously in *Journal of Feminist Family Therapy* (The Haworth Press, Inc.) Vol. 10, No. 1, 1998, pp. 23-47; and: *Transformations of Gender and Race: Family and Developmental Perspectives* (ed: Rhea V. Almeida) The Haworth Press, Inc., 1998, pp. 23-47. Single or multiple copies of this article are available for a fee from The Haworth Document Delivery Service [1-800-342-9678, 9:00 a.m. - 5:00 p.m. (EST). E-mail address: getinfo@haworthpressinc.com].

spect (tolerance as in acceptance of "other") others who are different, and negotiate (expanded identity) our interdependence with our environment and with our friends, partners, families, communities and society in ways which do not entail the exploitation.

KEY FACTORS IN THE MEASUREMENT
OF A CHILD'S MATURITY

- trust within the context of familiarity and difference
- interdependence within the context of multiple relationships
- tolerance: differentiation of self
- expanded identity within the context of diversity

The power to regain our own life comes from the discovery of the cosmic covenant, the deep harmony in the community of being in which we participate.

–Mary Daly

Unfortunately our Western mind, lacking all culture in this respect, has never yet devised a concept, nor even a name, for the 'union of opposites, through the middle path,' that most fundamental item of inward experience which could respectably be set against the Chinese concept of the Tao.

–Carl G. Jung

Developmental theory, the fundamental basis for formulations about human relationships, critically informs family theory and practice. The assessment of children of color is based upon psychological theories of health and adaptation taken from the dominant culture. These theories, based on narrow definitions of competence, are derived from andocentric (male-centered) ideals of development (Freud, 1905; Erikson, 1950; 1959; 1968; Kohlberg, 1969; 1981) and do not examine how the hidden assumptions embedded in our cultural discourses, social institutions, and individual psyches perpetuate male power and oppression. Such assumptions not only influence developmental theory, but shape our perceptions of social reality as therapists. Cultural context and communication, which are central to a child's development, are minimally acknowledged by family theory as it stands today.

In children's therapy, the child's sociocultural identity, racial and cultural history must be considered. For instance, in her reflections about origins of a Native American 'home,' Paula Gunn Allen (1992) says:

No Indian can grow to any age without being informed that her people were savages who interfered with progress pursued by respectable, loving, civilized, white people. We are the villains of the scenario when we are mentioned at all. We are absent from much of white history except when we are calmly, rationally, succinctly, and systematically dehumanized. On the few occasions we are noticed in any way other than as howling, bloodthirsty beings, we are acclaimed for our noble quaintness. In this definition, we are exotic curios. Our ancient arts and customs are used to draw tourist money to state coffers, into the pocketbooks and bank accounts of scholars, and into support of the American-in-Disneyland promoters' dream. (p. 49)

Such historical alteration of a child's racial and cultural story ignores a critical part of their identity, while overlooking the deleterious effects of such a portrayal upon a child's self-image. This distortion creates a narrow theoretical context for children's development: a context devoid of the realities of race, gender, class and culture.

Theories of life cycle development have acknowledged the various stages of family life (Carter & McGoldrick, 1989). Feminist studies have expanded developmental theory by informing therapists about the experiences of men and women within and outside of family life (Bem, 1993; Broverman, Broverman, Clarkson & Rosenkrantz, 1972; Bradley, 1985; Gilligan, Lyons & Hanmer, 1990). Theories of child development hold males as the standard, leaving the development of females invisible or on the periphery of our descriptions (Bem, 1993; 1983; Gilligan, 1982; Broverman, Vogel, Broverman, Clarkson & Rosenkrantz, 1972). On the whole, theories have left children of color out in the theoretical 'cold.'

White children, often the children of privilege, are not viewed as part of a continuum that is inclusive of diverse cultures. A continuum that upholds differences in cultures as contributing to developmental constructs of all children. Instead it is as if white children exist in isolation. Idealizing individuality and autonomy over human relatedness, logic over intuition, self-directed work disconnected from family life, and a general sense of entitlement, have left both privileged and disadvantaged children lacking. Traditional standards of healthy maturity have ignored the sense of emotional emptiness created by expectations of autonomy and separation. Such emphasis on individuality and autonomy contributes toward their emotional isolation. This creates skewed notions of maturity and lifelong dilemmas in intimate relationships (Kivel, 1992; Munroe, Munroe & Whiting, 1981). Autonomy then reflects in an immature sense of self and any connections supporting one's independence are masked as well. Maturity, within the skewed context of autonomy without intimate connections, ascribes to values of power for children of privilege. Kivel, for instance, challenges these symbols of power (autonomy and individuality), as problematic to the development of white male children. He adds that many of these symbols of power handed down from fathers to sons over generations are not necessarily the legacies that many fathers wish to pass on to their sons. Instead, legacies of autonomy within the context of human connectedness and collaboration may be the better informed messages to be shared with sons of the future.

Miller's (1984) concept of differentiation describes mature relationships as becoming increasingly more complex in their relatedness and ability to contain incongruities. Incongruities specific to gender differences. Absent from this analysis, however, is any description of power and differences surrounding race.

Standards for successful achievement are the same regardless of the resources available to children. Resources related to race or economic privilege, language fluency of the dominant culture, or community support are not differentiated as specific to academic outcome. For instance, successful attainment of academic behaviors, consonant with the dominant cultures' expectations, are achieved by mostly white male children, and fewer girls. These achievements are not linked to the many systems of support such as racial, economic and emotional resources, privileged school systems, and general access to resources that enhance learning, that the dominant culture affords white male children. These same standards are held up for children of color backgrounds. Lacking the supportive mechanisms of the hegemony, such children are successful within these traditional institutions only through the use of many other adaptive resources. These other adaptive resources, however, remain unexamined in the child development literature. In contrast, when these children do have difficulty negotiating success, the lack of societal structures in support of them is not recognized.

Schieffelin and Ochs (1986) emphasize the importance of language socialization as it relates to development. Children's learning of language helps inform them about relationships with family, friends, and society, and depends on a child's race, gender, class, and culture. Brice-Heath, (1988) describes this as follows:

Black families in the nineteenth and twentieth centuries have developed different patterns of language socialization as a result of their relative degrees of access and entry into particular class structures, employment opportunities, and religious networks. (p. 33)

The cultural variability of language socialization is a key factor in development and school performance is interrelated with historical, structural, familial and psychological factors.

REVIEW OF THE LITERATURE

Most developmental theories have in common their focus on a child's independence, ability to successfully compete with others, and high self esteem as defined by separateness (autonomy). These theories de-emphasize collaboration and connectedness. In addition, the literature is rich with feminist critique, which critiques these theories for overwhelmingly locating the source of a child's maladaptation at his/her deprivation of a need, usually described as something not met by the mother. Tyson (1986) describes the biases in developmental theory that stress abnormalities and deviations, instead of healthy adaptations, blame the mother for any problems, and view developmental experiences as consisting of concrete units. A few examples of these compartmentalized achievements are play and eating patterns, crawling, walking, talking, attending to directions and frustration tolerance. Feminist writings, however, have pointed to the excess responsibility placed on mothers, and the exclusion of responsibility on fathers (Goodrich, 1991; Hochschild & Machang, 1989; Maccoby, 1990; Steil & Weltman, 1991).

A brief reflection on traditional theory is noteworthy at this point. Erikson's (1963) contributions to theories of human development are widely used in training and clinical practice. His theory values and promotes competitive, hierarchical traits in young children, instead of encouraging differences that promote standards of collaboration. Erikson's theory specifically devalues the development of communication skills and ability to relate in favor of values of autonomy and self assertion (McGoldrick, 1989; 1995). His definition of tasks that are stage-specific, based on age and maturity, do not reflect life as an ongoing process of growth. In other words, we see psychological development as an ongoing process in which there are not developmental 'stages' to be completed, but rather, certain dimensions of healthy development are developed at an early age and expanded upon throughout the life cycle. Furthermore, differences across cultures account for variability in development with relation to age and maturity not accounted for in his definitions. While he recognizes that the self concept and self esteem of minority children is significantly affected by the stigma of membership in a devalued ethnic group (Taylor and Huang, 1989), this important observation is not incorporated into his developmental theory; this makes invisible the children of color. Erikson's

(1969) germinal work on Ghandi and the origins of militant nonviolence reflect a particular openness to understanding the evolution of human development and colonial oppression within another culture. Similarly, this work shows a detailed understanding of the Indian life cycle (dharmas) that differs for men and women. His analysis of Ghandi's life and the Indian cultural identity reflects his own efforts to embrace an Indian spirituality. However, this information does not appear to influence his conceptualization of both gender and culture with regard to children's developmental theory.

Critiques of Freud have offered some insights into his devaluing of women and misrepresentation of children. In critiquing Freud's idea about childhood seduction as primarily a fantasy rather than a remembrance of actual fact, Masson (1993) credits Freud with being rather enlightened, but then recants the idea. Masson further asserts this to be a failure of moral nerve–an accommodation to male authority and power at the expense of children. Gilman (1993), in his analysis of Freud's representation of race and gender, argues that Freud, as a Jew in a violently anti-Semitic world, perhaps dealt with anxiety about himself by casting it onto other cultural "inferiors"–such as women.

Piaget and Inhelder (1969) proposed the concrete stages of physical and cognitive development. This theory accounts for four major factors that influence development: (1) biological, (2) interactional factors, between the environment and cognitive structures, (3) interactional factors between the individual and their social context, universal for all societies, and (4) socio-cultural and education factors that are different among societies. Although Piaget's work has been widely used cross-culturally, there have been some problems in universal applicability (Nyiti, 1976). Some of these problems relate to differences in concept development and measurement between, for example, African and European children. Concepts such as play and relationships activities, language (fluency with several languages for African children versus monolinguism for European children), environmental circumstances such as illness, nutrition, cosmological influences of rituals and religious beliefs significantly alter African children's development of concepts (Hale-Benson, 1982).

Clearly, distinctions need to be made between psychobiological or maturational outcomes and cultural outcomes. These critical dimensions are frequently undifferentiated (Ogbu, 1988). Cross-cultural reports further indicate that populations in many Asian, Eskimo and non-European cultures vary in formal operational thinking (Dasen, 1977). In some populations, as in highly technologically advanced societies, cultural tasks require a fairly high degree of formal operational thinking, making this type of thinking valuable. In contrast, cultural tasks in other populations do not require much formal operational thinking, nor is it highly valued or promoted.

Other cross cultural studies that compare socialization patterns in Japan, China, Uganda and the United States challenge Americans' cultural biases and raise questions about this cultures' childrearing practices (Tobin, Wu, & Davidson, 1989; Ainsworth, 1967). They describe the importance of indulgence and protection of young children in Asian cultures. In contrast, independent thinking in Asian cultures is only encouraged within a context of respect and interconnectedness. This is intended to de-emphasize individuality as synonymous with autonomy and separation of self from others. The values of loyalty and caring for others are seen as more critical than individual achievements. For example 4-5 year old boys from Asian Indian families appear younger than their chronological age. This is because they are pampered and permitted freedom of movement and language until they reach 7 or 8 years of age. Their behavior can be viewed as "out of control" if assessed outside of an Asian Indian context of child-rearing practices. It should be noted however, that the above aspects of socialization have difficulties as well (Rolland, 1988). Lack of differentiation of self is as problematic as overemphasis on self. For instance, the dilemma created by nondifferentiation of self is an inability to separate one's own thoughts and decisions from those of the "collective" context. Healthy differentiation of self does not mean ignoring the context, but in fact being able to achieve one's desires while respecting the right of others to do the same; not focusing only on oneself nor entirely accepting the thinking put forth by the larger context. A balance of self in context is what these studies afford us.

Other relationships not explored in traditional theory include a child's relationship with different family members, with friends, caregivers, society at large, with her/his culture, and with different environments. Studies of children's self-image have questioned the validity of assumptions that deleterious life experiences of minority and "disadvantaged" children inhibit the acquisition of positive self images (Proshansky & Newton, 1968). Evidence has demonstrated that the self-images of these children are at least as positive as those of their wealthier, white counterparts (Rosenberg, 1979). Although the studies assumed these children to have adaptive strategies, these strategies were not explicated. The omitting of such strategies is a theme common to these studies. For example, young white children who are exposed to racially mixed caretakers are more comfortable in diverse situations and respectful towards professionals of color than if they are raised by their mothers in isolated contexts. In contrast, young children of color for the most part are taught early on that cooperation with all adults, whites in particular, is necessary for their success in life. This is one example of how hidden strategies of adaptation are obscured.

A number of studies point to the notion that early aspirations for most children are equally high. However, the aspirations of children of color decline as their knowledge about their racial/personal/familial/cultural selves intersect with larger systems that are infused with negative messages (Majors & Billson, 1992). This occurs mostly at about the time a child enters school, at around age four or five. These aspirations, in turn, have an effect on a child's self-image. In other words, all of the people and contexts in which a child operates are extremely important in her/his development. The family context itself is not sufficient to offset some of these external influences. Traditional developmental theory does not define communication as a pivotal aspect of this ongoing process of maturation.

Bem (1993, 1983), in her discussion of gender schema theory, describes a generalized readiness on the part of the child to encode and organize information (including that of the self) according to the culture's definitions of maleness and femaleness. The work of Gilligan and her colleagues (1991, 1990, 1988, 1982) demonstrate the major gaps that exist between formulations designed for male children (white) and those developmental life cycle issues relevant to female children. Gilligan's work is criticized on two accounts: (1) for portraying an idea that differences are intrinsically gender based, rather than responses to socialization patterns (Hare-Mustin, 1987) and (2) for the failure to acknowledge differences that exist between privileged versus impoverished communities (Gilligan, Rogers, & Tolman, 1991; Gilligan, Lyons & Hanmer, 1990; Gilligan, Ward, Taylor, & Bardige, 1988). These studies on diversity of race, class and gender were drawn from a prestigious girls school, thereby limiting the usefulness of generalizing from this information. Gilligan's (Gilligan et al., 1988) writings, however, are drawn from her experience with African-American children in inner cities. The class distinctions between this population and the children from privileged environments are not explicated. Gilligan, whose work has not gone uncriticized, does force us to question current moral assumptions. Her theory of morality has raised fundamental questions about notions of justice and caring as two critical dimensions in mature human development. Connections in caring for "other," in fairness to "self," are central to the development of a moral presence and the experience of justice (Gilligan, Lyons, & Hanmer, 1990). Phillips and Zigler (1980) emphasize the significance of socioeconomic status, ethnic group membership, and gender as among the powerful influences that organize children's development. Havighurst (1976) takes this point a step further in describing how a Black child's acquiescence to upper middle class norms might reflect more a process of submission than healthy development. Due to the impact of racism, "assimilating" to the norms of a white society has meant having to give up much of ones' own connectedness to race and culture. This is evidenced in manner of speaking, dress, music, communication and social distance from one's community.

The works of McAdoo (1993), Powell, Yamamoto, Romero, and Morales (1983), Ramirez and Castaneda (1974) and De Anda (1984) have articulated many of these gaps in Gilligan's work and described the range of differences in adaptation that exist for children that straddle two cultures while reaching for competence in both. Some of these resources are the ability to communicate in several languages and multiple contexts, to understand verbal and nonverbal cues, and to learn how to negotiate various systems. In a study of 4, 5, 6, and 7 year olds, Young-Shi Ou and McAdoo (1993) found upper-class children in African-American and Chinese communities to have clearer preferences in identification with their own race than lower-class children. Information regarding race preference was obtained from questions such as who they felt closer to, who they would rather be like, and who they would like to play with. Social class and ethnicity are two major influences of human development (Havighurst, 1976). These influences operate within a person's ecological life space interacting with family and friends, community and culture. Havighurst elaborates on class and ethnic distinctions:

> Thus in a consideration of social class as an ecological factor or set of forces in human development and behavior, ethnicity always stands at the side of the stage, ready to explain some of the phenomena which cannot be understood by social class considerations alone. (p. 57)

His model suggests that for upper-middle class European Jews, Japanese and Chinese Americans, ethnicity outweighs social class. By comparison, he suggests that for Blacks, South and East European ethnics, and Latinos/as, social class overrides ethnicity. Hale-Bensen (1982) argues against this analysis. She says that class, which is defined mostly by income and occupation in the dominant culture, does not reflect the larger context of socialization, which for African-Americans is transmitted through belief systems and values over several generations. African-American children from an upper-middle class nuclear family frequently receive much of their socialization from extended family members who would be considered lower-class. Moreover, in most other societies of the world it is less likely that a person moves class levels in one generation. This is an American phenomenon which has contributed in part to the myth of a "class-less" society.

Majors and Billson (1992) describe differences in a child's social environment that significantly influence class stability. They suggest that economic privilege and education of parents are critical buffers for children struggling to succeed. Clunis and Green (1988) describe the strategy of "armoring" as a critical adaptive resource of minority children and their parents to racial intolerance. The protective shield this affords them embraces healthy maturity. Greene (1992) refers to this adaptive process as racial socialization which, for African-American parents, is an integral part of child rearing. This adaptation involves the mastery of a multitude of tasks for the development of children of color and their families in the face of a dominant culture that is frequently hostile. The process of healthy adaptation within an antagonistic culture–a critical dimension of development for many children of color–is not acknowledged within the dominant developmental perspectives.

Similarly, Taylor-Gibbs and Huang (1989) discuss various developmental differences of children according to their race, ethnic background, and social class. Taylor-Gibbs et al. (1989) discuss how immigrant children are required to negotiate two worlds simultaneously: that of their own culture and that of the dominant culture. While straddling and moving back and forth between both cultures is stressful, it is also a great resource. Values of tolerance and connections amid diversity are only a few of the adaptations developed.

Also noteworthy is the way in which Gardner (1983) and Hale-Benson (1986) describe intelligence as part of a world view that is inclusive of a range of human potential such as language and communication, music and dance, bodily-kinesthics, logic and social skills. They urge the use of this broad view of intelligence in assessing the development of all children. For example, a 10 year old African American male child is referred to treatment because he appears to be depressed and highly distractible in the classroom over several weeks. In obtaining specifics as to exactly where he exhibits this behavior, his family reports that he is fine at home and in most of his classes except for the language arts class. In the language arts class they are learning to analyze classical music. He seems distracted and has great difficulty participating with a group of mostly White children. We suggested introducing music that might be more familiar to him. This was based on the assumption that the music was unfamiliar to him, and he was one of only three minority kids in a class of 24. When Michael Jackson was introduced as a way to differentiate this child's response to familiarity versus strangeness, he was animated and became an enthusiastic participant. Similarly, some of the other children who were less familiar with Michael Jackson appeared to perform less well.

RETHINKING THE DIMENSIONS OF CHILDHOOD DEVELOPMENT: A SELF IN CONTEXT

In every society, race, gender, class and culture (RGCC) form a basic structure within which individuals learn what behaviors, beliefs, values and ways of relating to others they will be expected to demonstrate throughout life. It is this context which carries every child from birth and childhood through adulthood to death and defines her or his legacy for the next generation. The racial, gender, class and cultural structure of any society profoundly influences the parameters of a child's evolving ability to share, negotiate and communicate. It prescribes his or her way of being interdependent with others. RGCC is the foundation from which a child's development is assessed and treatment is provided.

Our RGCC construct includes a child's evolution in ability to share, negotiate, and communicate on multiple levels. It further holds valuable the interdependence in relationships, respect for others regardless of social status, and a curiosity about difference with respect to race, gender, class and culture (Almeida, Woods, Messineo, & Font, 1998). Healthy maturity is ascertained by the culture's repertoire of competencies and the indigenous formulas by which those culturally diverse competencies are socialized. Competence is defined as the capacity to speak a language and get things done in a manner deemed acceptable by the members of one's own culture (Ogbu, 1981). Thus, a child's development consists of acquisition of the cognitive, communicative, motivational, social-emotional and affective competencies specific to the race, gender, class and culture context. Healthy maturity for all children depends on embracing one's own uniqueness in the context of connections around differences of others. Furthermore, the ability to experience a breadth of emotions is positively correlated to intellectual development. It is our belief that healthy exposure to diversity further expands one's emotional maturity thereby increasing the level of intellectual development. Social contexts are very much the essence of how children grow and learn. Repertoires of self learning and connections to others occur with children who are in concert with their social context of RGCC. For instance, girls' capacity for flexibility in relationships offers important ideals to hold for maturation for all children. Boys' ability to reason and use logic can add to maturation. Similarly, the tenacity with which children from diverse cultures navigate complexity is important learning for all children. In our clinical work we have boys and girls describe in detail their daily skills that we validate and then to borrow from one another in order to broaden their levels of adaptation and maturity. Similarly, we emphasize the numerous skills that children from diverse cultures perform on a daily basis that are taken for granted. For example, a 9 year old Chinese girl whose peers marvel at the fact that she can do her homework in a common room with 8-10 family members and younger children playing. The concept of "quiet" is neither a value nor an option in many homes. Similarly, in a continued spirit of support towards children's openness to difference we introduce a variety of foods to children in our sessions, sensitizing them to differences in taste, smell and texture. The experiencing of each child bringing in snacks and trying each other's foods helps them to build trust and tolerance. While most immigrant and minority children eat food from the dominant culture, most White children do not experiment with differences in food until later in life.

Children are raised in a society which very quickly assigns roles and expectations based on gender, race, and class. Thus, we must realize that RGCC competencies are not simply milestones that children reach individually, but accomplishments that evolve within a complex web of racial, cultural and familial contexts. The examining of strengths from diverse cultures contributes greatly to expansions of human development.

It is our belief that children are best able to develop their full potential, emotionally, intellectually, physically and spiritually, when they are exposed in positive ways to diversity and encouraged to embrace it. We would hypothesize that children who are least restricted by rigid gender, cultural, or class role constraints are likely to develop the most evolved sense of self in context.

Development must be defined by more than intellectual performance, analytical reasoning ability, and ability to think of one's functioning as autonomous and self determined. Ogbu's studies (1981) demonstrate that the intellectual tasks which Western theorists such as Piaget have used as definers of maturity are extraordinarily narrow indicators of intelligence and totally inadequate as a schema for understanding the rich possibilities of a child's intellectual development.

THE MYTH OF AUTONOMY AND SELF-DETERMINATION

Those with the most privilege in our society–especially those who are white and male and who have financial and social status–tend to be systematically kept unconscious of their dependence on others. They remain completely unaware of the hidden ways in which our society supports their so-called "autonomous" functioning. Thus, many white men who benefited from the GI bill to attain their education now consider it a form of welfare to provide for the education of minorities of the current generation.

DEVELOPING A MATURE INTERDEPENDENT SELF

We believe that maturity depends on seeing past these myopic myths of autonomy and self-determination. It requires that we appreciate our basic interdependence on each other and on nature. Viewed from this perspective, maturity involves skill such as:

1. Trust–or feeling safe in the context of the familiar and the unfamiliar or different.
2. Interdependence–the ability to relate in the context of others.
3. Tolerance–the ability to accept one's self, while simultaneously accepting differences in others; to maintain one's values and beliefs while relating generously to others. This sense of relating to others upholds values in the sense of community and respect for her/histories with a consciousness of past, present and future life (not forgetting that the Native Americans were owners of this land, and that African Americans were brought here as slaves, would be examples of respecting a history of the past).
4. Expanded identities–ability to acknowledge our own expanded identities in the context of diversity–namely, all of the skills that come from living intimately in two or more cultures simultaneously.

1. Trust Within the Context of Familiarity and Difference

Infants and toddlers begin developing trust in their immediate environment, which ideally supports their safety and development. Developing trust involves orienting oneself to one's cultural group and its position in the world. Obviously, this task of developing trust is more difficult if you come from a group that is stigmatized by the wider society. How do you learn basic trust if you are a member of a group that is hated for the color of their skin, the shape of their eyes, their religious beliefs or the way they walk? Obviously, a child of color who develops a sense of basic trust has done something more remarkable than a white child who comes to the same trust. Our theories of child development must take this fact into account. An African proverb about raising children says "It takes a village to raise a child."

Children's sense of security evolves through their connection and identification with those who care for them–mothers, fathers, siblings, nannies, baby-sitters, grandparents, aunts, uncles and all the others who participate in their caretaking. Traditional formulations of child development have ignored this rich context and offered us the paucity of a one dimensional lens for viewing a child's development: the mother-child relationship. In most cultures throughout history mothers have not been the primary caretakers of their children, since they were usually busy with other work. Grandparents and other elders as well as older siblings have, for the most part, been the primary caretakers of children. When we focus so myopically on the role of mothers we are blinded to the richness of environments in which children generally grow up. We necessarily invalidate these contexts by ignoring them, and thus become unable to see, and therefore to encourage, many of the major influences on children as they develop. Only if we expand our lens to a child's full environment can we properly measure the characteristics which may help them attain their full potential.

Developing a Self in a Non-Affirming Environment

It takes great maturity to be able to develop one's sense of self in an unfamiliar setting, where one has little support than it does in a context where everyone in the outside world affirms your values. Those in the dominant groups of our society receive this affirmation daily, whereas many others do not grow up with this affirmation of their "selfhood": a gay or lesbian child, a disabled child, a girl, a child of color, or a poor child. These children are not the ones depicted in books and movies as the "valued" child. Thus, a non-privileged child who does manage to develop a strong "self" has accomplished a great developmental feat, whereas a child who has always been affirmed may more easily internalize this security. In fact, healthy development requires establishing a solid sense of our unique selves in the context of our connections to others. Those who are privileged develop connections amidst a web of disassociations. It is the privilege, however, that maintains their buffered position; maintaining the ideal of autonomy through the illusion of separateness and disassociation. Connecting to others becomes a particular challenge when they are different. Thus, the most challenging aspect of development involves our negotiation of interface with others who are different from ourselves: men and women; young and old; black, brown, yellow and white; wealthy and poor; heterosexual and homosexual.

Children's development is more multifarious than our theories have indicated. Because our society so quickly assigns roles and expectations based on gender, culture, class and race, children's competencies are obviously not simply milestones that they reach individually, but rather accomplishments that evolve within a complex web of racial, cultural and familial contexts. The constraints of a particular social context necessarily circumscribe a child's acquisition of cognitive, communicative, motivational, social, emotional and affective skills. Thus, our evaluation of these abilities can only be meaningful if these constraints are taken into account.

While infants are not able to distinguish racial characteristics, there is a general context of familiarity related to sounds, rhythm and smells (early language communication). Studies that examine social-cognitive development and toys state that toys play a major role in gender and race socialization across socioeconomic groups beginning in late infancy (Bradley, 1985). Toys, dolls, games, books, music and foods emphasize a child's cultural background. Communication that embraces differences among cultures rather than imposing dominant values is central to a child's ability to develop trust within and outside of the family.

2. Interdependence Within the Context of Relationships

The ability to communicate within a context that reinforces a child's sense of self, in relation to her/his culture and environment, is critical to her/his healthy development. The concept of interdependence applies to the ability to thrive and differentiate within cultures and between cultures. Acceptance of different styles of communication is one of the major links to the mature development of interdependence.

Style as a process of learning is related to interdependence. It defines how children "take in" information and then "express" it. The recognition of different styles is critical to the enhancement of distinct forms of communication within a context of diversity. Styles consist of analytical/rational types (mostly boys) on one end to relational/emotional (mostly girls) at the other end. For example we measure flexibility by a child's ability to respond to cross-gender and cross cultural activities. For example, a girl who prides herself on helping others in a group should also be able to focus on herself and express her difficulties. The counterpart of that example would be the ability of a White boy to listen to others in the group, give appropriate feedback and also describe his own difficulties in a respectful and non-blaming manner. We might have a minority child describe how respect is a necessary and valuable part of communication in his/her family life thereby elevating the notion of respect over self-centeredness.

Hale-Bensen (1986) describes behavioral styles as the framework from which one views the world: for instance, expression in relation to language, music, dance, religion, art, work, problem-solving, sports, writing, or any other area related to human expression. Style is important as it is the link to one's cultural group, making every style relevant and important to the functioning of a whole society.

White children are naturally born into a world where their own behavioral style of communication is emphasized. Styles such as the use of linear language, minimal use of body language, preference for written expression with seeing the world in parts rather than whole are common to white children. This is reflected in the expression of dance and music. These children are also continually exposed to reflections of their own images as effectively functioning and admired members of their society so that reinforcement of these images occurs early on. Books, movies, and public pictures mostly reflect children who are White. Silvern, Surbeck, Kelley, Williamson, and Taylor (1984) describe the vulnerability of young children in their ability to differentiate reality in the context of dominant imaging. Thus, children typically think what they see of these images in books, television, movies or the media, are real. They describe a study in which children of mixed race and gender were asked about the race of the "real" Santa Claus, before and after being presented with a Black Santa Claus. Findings reveal that the children, who initially reported that Santa was white, changed their opinion and reported that the "real" Santa was Black after being presented with a Black Santa. Children can be easily influenced by views of interdependence if this is the dominant perspective.

In clinical sessions we ask children to bring in pictures and stories of children different from themselves, regardless of what the presenting problem is. This continuous bridging of narratives provides the holding context for addressing a child's problem. This allows for the notion of problem resolution through connection rather than compartmentalization. Hale-Benson (1986) has developed a useful framework for thinking about the experiences of African-American children:

1. Sociocentric view of the world—one that looks at the whole instead of the parts.
2. Language with a wide use of coined interjections—use of Black language.
3. Expression of self through affective use of body language, systematic use of nuances and intonation, such as eye movement and positioning, preference for spontaneity.
4. Reliance on words that depend upon context for meaning with little meaning outside of their context—so preference for inferential reasoning rather than deductive or inductive reasoning.

5. Preference for oral-aural modalities for learning rather than "word" dependency in communication.
6. Tendency toward altruism, sense of justice and a preferred focus on people and their activities rather than on things. (p. 43)

In contrast, Asian cultures emphasize the following values in their child-rearing:

1. Cultural belonging that places great value on connections to others.
2. Emphasis on the value of tolerance and nonviolence.
3. Reliance on symbols that define context and communicate order.
4. Willingness to cooperate.
5. Feelings of loyalty towards others.

While generalizations can be pernicious, they are necessary to obtain a categorical reading about differences. The values described reflect developmental patterns central to the maturity of African-American and Asian children. Many of these dimensions are useful in enhancing the development of all children. With respect to fluency in reading and writing of literature, for instance, comprehension requires the reading of William Shakespeare and Emily Dickinson as well as James Baldwin, Carlos Fuentes, Paula Gunn Allen, V. S. Naipal, and Mukherjee. While these readings might appear to be advanced literature, they ought to be a central part of early language arts.

Gilligan, Ward, Taylor, and Bardige (1988) write on perspectives of self, relationships and morality:

> The connected self is grounded in interdependence which comes from recognition of the interconnectedness of people. (p. 33)

Interdependence is a critical dimension of healthy psychological development. A continuum of skills relative to interdependence includes cooperative play, expression of a full range of emotions and tolerance of such emotions in self and others, expression of nurturing and caretaking, use of different forms of play, and involvement with a variety of athletic activities. The value of interconnectedness is particularly significant to rebalancing male/female patterns of socialization.

3. Tolerance: Differentiation of Self

Tolerance is essentially a value that embraces difference with respect. Tolerance by the dominant culture, within the context of childhood development, is the acknowledgment of the disparity that exists among different racial, gender, class and cultural backgrounds. Beyond this acknowledgment is understanding the significance of embracing difference at a personal level for all children. This type of curiosity about "others" creates a social context of tolerance. What is masked in this conception of human development is the unique experience of women, and those who are racially, sexually or culturally different. This remains an important structural omission. The absence of language in describing such a critical phenomenon results in clinical translations that continue to disempower women and the racially and culturally different. For example, a 14 year old boy, Suyam, of Chinese and Turkish heritage, but visibly Chinese looking, was referred for failing grades, and alcohol and drug use. He presented angrily, and the referring therapist indicated that his parents were "enabling" him, and that his immature "acting-out" in the classroom contributed to the negativity in teacher-responsiveness and thus his failing grades. The parents were labeled as resistant and refusing to cooperate with the school officials and therapy. In exploring the family's past with therapeutic suggestion, they reported attending Al-Anon and Al-Ateen for one year with their entire family, including Suyam. They seemed cooperative and willing to try anything for their son. As a Chinese man, Suyam's father was distressed with the idea from Al-Anon that he not be responsible for his son's behavior. He felt it was his obligation to take care of his son. The language of over and underresponsibility in the addictions field was contextualized to fit this family's definitions of caretaking, communication and spirituality. They could incorporate aspects of the AA model into their life but could not, and rightly so, give up their entire cultural belief system to privilege the addictions model. Furthermore, the entire family experienced hidden dimensions of racism in the school that they were unable to define. Upon closer examination it was apparent that Suyam was poorly treated in a number of instances in the classroom as well as by the principal. Once again, his reactivity if only viewed with Bowen's definition of human development leaves out the power of the context to strongly impact his emotional response and hence his maturational development. A recontextualizing of Suyam's problem while simultaneously advocating on his behalf in the school brought forth the desired outcome. He improved academically and entirely gave up use of drugs and alcohol.

Dimensions of healthy development for children includes communication about differences with respect to race, gender, class and culture, and an opportunity to incorporate cross-cultural styles of relating. This early recognition of difference will become more important in early adolescence when many white children may for the first time see the ways in which they are different from their peers. For example, white adolescents who think they are gay or lesbian may for the first time be faced with a difference which isolates them. Or, in contrast, a white male adolescent might for the first time come in personal contact with a black male or female adolescent who he is unsure how to relate to.

Many non-western cultures believe that human development is fundamentally connected to all of life: the sacredness of and respect for the aesthetics of nature, respect for the land, harmony with the environment and a strong sense of continuity for the history of the world and thereby of culture and family.

By laying the framework for acceptance and celebration of difference, children will more easily accept and connect to others, as well as to aspects of themselves that are different. A sense of spiritual continuity in human connectedness ultimately binds all ties (Orenstein, 1990).

4. Expanded Identities in the Context of Diversity

A continuous challenge exists for children developing within the context of race, gender, class and culture (RGCC). In a diverse society, expanded identities are a tremendous resource. For instance, all boys can reach toward a more relational and less self focused sense of self. This includes relationships based on nurturance and care for others and self. Friendships between all boys and girls can be embellished throughout the lifecycle, as in other cultures. These friendships can serve to challenge many of this cultures' dominant ideas regarding separateness and difference.

Boys of all races may benefit from learning styles that are less problem solving, solution-oriented, and logic-centered, and more oriented towards understanding context and its parts in relation to the problem. Our society must teach boys that "success" needs to occur in a context of shared power.

Girls of all races in contrast can benefit from establishing an identity which allows them to make choices that are more independent and self related, associated with the anxiety of disappointing "others." This entails a particular clarity and decisiveness regarding their own values, in multiple contexts. Embracing their achievements, in conjunction with relationships adds a rich dimension.

Similarly girls of color (and those from lower socioeconomic groups) require support in assuming leadership roles with plans for economic independence, to create a balance with the overt and covert training that white boys receive. These children experience intense feelings of isolation when their identities are trimmed to fit the dominant culture. It is essential that they be encouraged to make choices that strengthen their cultural identification and invite their participation within the larger culture. Their struggle with identity is twofold. Coupled with the disregard for their culture is the pressure to conform to values of the dominant culture. Their identity exists in multiple contexts and can be celebrated that way.

Cultures based on ritual tradition, like those of many American Indian and Asian cultures, operate on assumptions quite different from western patriarchal cultures. These cultures believe in the connectedness of humankind with the universe, a respect for nonhuman life forms and aesthetic beauty, and an acceptance of a supernatural existence. Notions of power in many of these cultures is based on the wisdom of age, and connections of multiple familial and community relationships. Age takes on entirely different meaning in relation to children's development. Power through the acquisition of material goods and status is not central to harmony in relationships in many of these cultures. Incorporating these differences in world views are important to the RGCC matrix of children's development.

We model diversity for our clients through the diversity of our own staff, which is structured intentionally to attend to this modeling aspect of development. When staff are not available we use college students and parents who have a raised consciousness about diversity, to counter all of the hierarchical segregation based on race, gender, class and culture. Our clinical context integrates all of these rigid categories and includes children of varying ages–the intent is for older children (boys in particular) to learn to care for younger children and listen attentively to them, increasing their tolerance in social situations. We have girls and children of color assume roles of leadership in a way that enables them to experience a sharing of power with their white counterparts. In addition to written questionnaires that we use to elicit information, we use the age mixes to discuss the value of grandparents and the aged in general, to provide a counterpart of youth as the predominant measure of life.

A SAMPLE CASE

A 38 year old Italian, recently separated woman brings her two sons, 7 and 11, for therapy. She is in the midst of a recent separation from her husband who has been peripherally involved with the children through their marriage. The younger boy was suspended for choking another child on the playground. The presenting problem is her concern, and that of the teachers, that Michael, 11, is violent towards other children and towards his brother as well. She has taken the children to many therapists. Michael carries the label ADHD, hyperactive, and has been on medication intermittently, without any results. The mother is the principal of a daycare facility having received her education as a child development specialist at Bank Street, New York. The prior therapies were a mixture of expression through play, talking about feelings, and behavior modification contracts. The mother was seen in a few more collateral sessions than the children's father, who served in the marines and was now working in real estate. We were not successful in engaging this father in treatment. He was skeptical about whether therapy could change anything. The boys were introduced in separate culture circles (groups of same sex children of varying ages, race and class backgrounds and cultures) to issues of gender, race, class and culture. They were instructed to replace any disrespectful language with respectful alternatives. There were older boys in these circles acting as mentors (sponsors) who both initiated the newcomers into this process and assisted them with different ways of being with one another. With the help of the therapists, the boys were read stories of warriors who used the courage of love, caring, and respect instead of the fist or sword; *Charlotte's Web*, *The Land Before Time*, and *Corina Corina*, addressed themes of loss; *Ariel the Mermaid*, and *Beauty and the Beast* addressed gender role socialization and its assaultive impact on young boys and girls. The violence that Michael inflicted on others was gradually deconstructed throughout this matrix of RGCC that grew around him, his brother and mother. His father was only present through drawings and conversation. Behavioral child/parent charts were used to reinforce the children's cooperation around non-violence and support the mother's efforts in the home. However, these were not the continuous nor major focus. While the mother experienced no violence from her husband, nor did either parent use violence in disciplining the children, the children spent much after school and weekend time at their grandparents' home, unsupervised. They watched hours of violence on television, with no consistent nurturance, and were simultaneously being reinforced on the playground for adopting rigid norms of masculinity.

CONCLUSION

The RGCC construct of developmental theory offers a link between evolving theories and practice of feminist thought, cultural diversity and family therapy. Our view of human development is inclusive of race, gender,[1] class and culture. We provide a context within which children and their families/caretakers can develop a heightened sense of racial, gender, class and cultural consciousness. Within this quilt of consciousness they find a range of solutions to the problems that brought them to us. The measurement of a person's maturity includes four key factors:

- trust/safety within the context of familiarity and difference
- interdependence within the context of multiple relationships
- tolerance: differentiation of self
- expanded identity within the context of diversity

Children are born into this society with many of the same aspirations for learning and growth, but with different resources both within and outside of their family life. The purpose of this framework is to assist therapists and educators in acknowledging and stretching for the adaptive resources that children of diverse groups have developed in their cultures of origin, while simultaneously countering the privilege of white children and the celebration of the compartmentalized self prominent in all of child development theory. Secure and healthy development for our children in the future requires intricate bridging with evolving contexts and complexities of race, gender, class, and culture (RGCC) for all children in families.

NOTE

1. We hope that through the dismantling of rigid roles of masculinity and femininity there will be space for the normal evaluation of gays and lesbians.

REFERENCES

Almeida, R., Woods, Messineo, T., & Font, R. (1998). The Cultural Context Model: A Socioeducational Approach to Family Intervention. *Re-Visioning Family Therapy: Culture, Class, Race, and Gender,* edited by Monica McGoldrick, Guilford Publication, New York.

Ainsworth, M.D. (1967). Infancy in Uganda: infant care and the growth of love. Baltimore, Maryland: The Johns Hopkins University Press.

Bem, S.L. (1983). Gender schema theory and its implications for child development. Signs, 8 (4), pp. 598-616.

Bem, S.L. (1993). The Lenses of gender. Transforming the debate on sexual inequality. New Haven, Connecticut:Yale University Press.

Bradley, R. (1985). Social-cognitive development and education. Topics in Early Childhood Special Education, 5 (3), pp. 11-29.

Brice-Heath, S. (1988). Language socialization. New Directions for Child Development, 42, pp. 29-41.

Broverman, I., Vogel, S., Broverman, D., Clarkson, F., & Rosenkrantz, P. (1972). Sex-role stereotypes: A current appraisal. Journal of Social Issues, 28, pp. 58-78.

Carter, E.A. & McGoldrick, M. (1980). The family life cycle: A framework for family therapy. New York: Gardner Press.

Clunis, D.M. & Green, G.D. (1988). How racism defines couples in Clunis and Green (Eds.), Lesbian Couples-Seattle, Washington: Seal Press.

De Anda, D. (1984). Bicultural socialization: factors affecting the minority experience. Social Work, March-April, pp. 101-107.

Dasen, P. (1977). Piagetian psychology: Cross-cultural contributions. New York: Gardner Press.

Erikson, E.H. (1969). Ghandi's truth: on the origins of militant nonviolence. New York: W.W. Norton & Co., Inc.

Erikson, E.H. (1968). Identity: youth and crisis. New York: W.W. Norton. J. Strachey (Ed. 2nd Trans.).

Erikson, E.H. (1963). Childhood and society (2nd ed.). New York: W.W. Norton.

Erikson, E.H. (1959). Identity and the life cycle: selected papers. Psychological Issues: Monograph 1. New York: International Universities Press.

Erikson, E.H. (1950). Childhood and society. New York: W.W. Norton, Inc.

Freud, S. (1953). Three essays on the theory of sexuality. The standard edition of the complete psychological works of Sigmund Freud. London: Hogarth Press. (Original work published 1905)

Gardner, H. (1983). Frames of mind: the theory of multiple intelligences. New York: Basic Books.

Gilligan, C., Rogers, A.G., & Tolman, D.L. (1991). Women, girls, and psychotherapy: Reframing resistance. Binghamton, New York: Harrington Park Press.

Gilligan, C., Lyons, N.P., & Hanmer, T.J. (1990). Making connections: the relational worlds of adolescents girls at Emma Willard School. Cambridge, Massachusetts: Harvard University Press.

Gilligan, C., Ward, J.V., & Taylor, J., & Bardige, B. (1988). Mapping the moral Domain. Cambridge, Massachusetts: Harvard University Press.

Gilligan, C. (1982). In a different voice. Cambridge: Harvard University.

Gilman, S.L. (1993). Freud, race, and gender. Princeton: Princeton University Press.

Goodrich, T.J. (Ed.), (1991). Women and Power: Perspectives for Family Therapy. New York: W.W. Norton.

Greene, B. (1992). Racial socialization: A tool in psychotherapy with African American children. In L.A. Vargas & J.D. Koss-Chioino (Eds.). Working with culture: Psychotherapeutic interventions with ethnic minority youth (pp. 63-81). San Francisco, California: Jossey-Bass.

Gunn-Allen, P. (1992). The sacred hoop: recovering the feminine in American Indian tradition. Boston, Massachusetts: Beacon Press.

Hale-Benson, J.E. (1986). Black children–their roots, culture, and learning styles. Baltimore, Maryland: The Johns Hopkins University Press.

Hare-Mustin, R. (1992). Changing women, changing therapies: Clinical implications of the changing role of women. Journal of Feminist Family Therapy, 4 (3 & 4), 7-18.

Havighurst, R. (1976). The relative importance of social class and ethnicity. *Human Development*, 19, pp. 56-64.

Hochschild, A., with Machang, A. (1989). The Second Shift: Working Parents and the Revolution at Home. New York: Viking.

Kivel, P. (1992). Men's work: how to stop the violence that tears our lives apart. New York: Random House, Inc.

Kohlberg, L. (1969). Stage and Sequence: The cognitive developmental approach to socialization. In D. Goslin (Ed.). The handbook of socialization theory and research. Chicago, Illinois: Rand McNally.

Kohlberg, L. (1981). The philosophy of moral development: Moral stages and the idea of justice: Essays on moral development, 1. San Francisco, California: Harper & Row.

Maccoby, E.E. (1990). Gender and relationships: A developmental account. American Psychologist, 45, 513-520.

Majors, R. & Billson, J.M. (1992). Cool pose: The dilemmas of black manhood in America. New York: Lexington.

Masson, J.M. (1993). My father's guru: a journey through spirituality and disillusionment. Reading, Massachusetts: Addison-Wesley Publishing Co.

McAdoo, H. (1993). Family ethnicity: Strength in diversity. Newburg Park, California: Sage.

Miller, J.M. (1976). Toward a new psychology of women. Boston: Beacon Press.

Munroe, R., Munroe, R., & Whiting, J. (1981). Male sex-role resolutions. In R. Munroe, R. Munroe, and B. Whiting (Eds.). Handbook of cross-cultural human development. New York: STM Press.

Nyiti, R.M. (1976). The development of conservation in the Meru children of Tanzania. Child development, 47, pp. 1122-1129.

Ogbu, J.U. (1988). Black children and poverty: A developmental perspective cultural diversity and human development in New Directions for Child Development, No. 42, pp. 11-28. San Francisco, California: Jossey-Bass Inc.

Ogbu, J.U. (1981). Origins of human competence: A cultural-ecological perspective. Child Development, 52 (1), pp. 413-429.

Orenstein, G.F. (1990). Artists as healers: envisioning life-giving culture. In I. Diamond & G.F. Orenstein (Eds.). Reweaving the world–the emergence of ecofeminism. San Francisco, California: Sierra Club Books.

Ou, Y. & Pipes McAdoo, H. (1993). Socialization of Chinese American children. In Pipes McAdoo, H. Family ethnicity: strength in diversity. Newbury Park, California: Sage Publications.

Phillips & Zigler (1980). Children's self-image disparity: effects of age, socioeconomic status, ethnicity, and gender. Journal of Personality and Social Psychology, 39 (4), pp. 689-700.

Piaget, J. & Inhelder, R. (1969). The psychology of the child. New York: Basic books.

Powell, G.J., Yamamoto, J., Romero, A., & Morales, A. (1983). Psychosocial development of minority group children. New York: Brunner-Mazel.

Proshansky, H. & Newton, P. (1968). The nature and meaning of Negro self-identity. In M. Deutsch, I. Katz, & J. Jenson (Eds.). Social class, race, and psychological development. New York: Holt, Rinehart, & Winston.

Ramirez, M. & Castaneda, A. (1974). Cultural democracy, bi-cognitive development, and education. New York: Academic Press.

Roland, A. (1988). In search of self in India and Japan: toward a cross-cultural psychology. Princeton, NJ: Princeton University Press.

Rosenberg, M. (1979). Conceiving the self. New York: Basic Books.

Schieffelin, B.B. & Ochs, E. (1986). Language socialization. Annual Review of Anthropology, 15, pp. 163-191.

Silvern, S., Surbeck, E., Kelley, M.F., Williamson, P.A., Silvern, L.R., & Taylor, J. (1984). The role of racial identity constancy of children's perceptions. Journal of Social Psychology, 122 (2), pp. 223-226.

Steil, J.M., and Weltman, K. (1991). Marital inequality: The importance of resources, personal attributes, and social norms on career valuing and the allocation of domestic responsibilities. Sex Roles, 24, 161-179.

Taylor Gibbs, J. & Nahme Huang, L. (1989). Children of color: Psychological interventions with minority youth. San Francisco, CA: Jossey-Bass.

Tobin, J.J., Wu, D.Y.H., & Davidson, D.H. (1989). Preschool in three cultures–Japan, China and the United States. New Haven, Connecticut: Yale University Press.

Tyson, R. (1986). The roots of psychopathology and our theories of development. Journal of the American Academy of Child Psychiatry, 25 (1), pp. 12-23.

Evolving Constructs of Masculinity: Interviews with Andres Nazario, Jr., William Doherty, and Roberto Font: Commentary

Claudia Bepko
Rhea V. Almeida
Theresa Messineo
Yanella Stevenson

Dominant notions of masculinity prescribe ways of being for men that are as constricting and politically nuanced as those that define female behavior. Current studies of masculinity and its social construction have evolved largely in reaction to the feminist critique of the early men's movement. Some of the cultural representations of that movement included father's rights groups and the mythopoetic "return to manhood" drive that was fueled primarily by the writing of Robert Bly. The more current wave of what could be loosely referred to as the "men's movement" is represented in part by a group referred to as NOMAS–The National Organization of Men Against Sexism. This group embraces a

Claudia Bepko, MSW, is in Private Practice, Brunswick, ME. Rhea V. Almeida, PhD, is Founder and Executive Director, Institute for Family Services, 3 Clyde Road, Suite, 101, Somerset, NJ 08873 and Faculty Member, Family Institute of New Jersey, Metuchen, NJ. Theresa Messineo, LCSW, is Co-Director, Institute for Family Services, Somerset, NJ. Yanella Stevenson, LCSW, is in Private Practice, Somerset, NJ.

[Haworth co-indexing entry note]: "Evolving Constructs of Masculinity: Interviews with Andres Nazario, Jr., William Doherty, and Roberto Font: Commentary." Bepko, Claudia et al. Co-published simultaneously in *Journal of Feminist Family Therapy* (The Haworth Press, Inc.) Vol. 10, No. 1, 1998, pp. 49-79; and: *Transformations of Gender and Race: Family and Developmental Perspectives* (ed: Rhea V. Almeida) The Haworth Press, Inc., 1998, pp. 49-79. Single or multiple copies of this article are available for a fee from The Haworth Document Delivery Service [1-800-342-9678, 9:00 a.m. - 5:00 p.m. (EST). E-mail address: getinfo@haworthpressinc.com].

position of equality for women, gays, and lesbian women, and is strongly anti-racist. However, like the feminist movement, it lacks a position on inclusivity for men of diverse cultural backgrounds (Denborough, 1994).

The evolution of these social organizations focused on men's rights has been paralleled by the development in academia of the study of "masculinities." While it evolved essentially in reaction to the feminist critique, the study of masculinity and the attempt to reconstruct maleness has become a largely separate ideology.

The purpose of this paper is to examine men's evolving strivings to embody masculine ideals and to explore the varied constructions of masculinity that exist among men from various cultures. The developing scholarship of the men's movement has an important influence on the ongoing construction of women's roles. Since one's sense of gender is interactional and since masculinity is defined in a heterosexist context that presumes a complementary femininity, an understanding of evolving definitions of the masculine is critical to an accurate perception of what it means to be female in this culture. To date, family therapy theory and practice have not been informed by concepts of masculinity in a way that parallels the use of the feminist lens to deconstruct women's status in families.

In this paper, we will briefly discuss various assumptions and constructions of masculinity and the problems they pose for men of differing cultures. For purposes of this discussion, we define culture as the legacy of customs, traditions and ways of belonging to family and community life of a particular group of people: the arts, beliefs, customs, institutions and all other products of human work and thought created by that particular group.

We prefer not to interiorize culture as specific to a particular individual or family, but rather to describe the larger processes of culture as they intersect with patriarchy, colonization, racism, capitalism and anti-Semitism and thereby affect a given group, family or individual. Oppression and violence, for instance, happen within the interior interactions of a family, couple, or group, but they represent the influence of beliefs embedded in the mores of the larger culture.

We have asked three male family therapists of different cultural and racial backgrounds to offer a commentary on their own evolving notions of masculinity and to outline the ways they would bring those constructions, as well as issues of race, sexual orientation and culture, into the therapy, even when those concerns are not part of the presenting problem. Finally, four female family therapists respond to the men, concluding with a discussion of the clinical implications of a focus on masculinity and its intersection with issues of race, class, sexual orientation and culture.

MASCULINITY AND DIFFERENCE

Like its feminist counterpart, one of the major weaknesses of the masculinities movement in academia is its tendency to obscure the differences between white men and men of color, men of privilege and working class men, older men and young men, and heterosexual men and gay men of all races. Racism, sexism, and sexual orientation across cultures interweave to create different expressions of masculinity among men from diverse backgrounds. Furthermore, the global relationship between men in capitalist countries and those in third world countries has received no attention in this analysis. Robert Jay Green's *Traditional Norms of the Male Role* (Green, 1998) outlines the core elements of hegemonic masculinity. These include avoidance of childcare and other nurturing activities because of their association with women's roles, avoidance of emotional closeness with other men, making work more a priority than family connections, restriction of emotionality except for expression of anger, striving for dominance and control within relationships, the use of anger as a primary means for conflict resolution, the objectification of women through a non-relational attitude towards sexuality, and homophobia. These role prescriptions into which all men are socialized (with some variations cross-culturally) are like a primer which lays the attitudinal and institutional foundation for male control in a range of settings.

These prescriptions, grounded as they are in white, middle-class sensibilities, create particular dilemmas for men of color. For example, Majors and Billison (1992) and McCall (1995) describe the ways that institutional racism limits opportunities for African American men to fulfill the dominant prescription that men prove their masculinity by achieving high incomes and prestigious positions within the world of work. The simultaneous demand for work performance and exclusion from the opportunity to fulfill that demand generates frustration, rage, desperation, and an array of other emotions. Men of color know that there is little public recognition for their predicament and that any expression of their feelings of frustration and rage is only likely to stir some form of heightened institutional coercion by the white establishment. Consequently, African American men may adopt very rigidified expressions of masculinity such as "gansta rap" and the participation in suicide missions in Desert Storm. "Playing it cool becomes the mask of choice" (Majors and Billison, 1992). More important is the reality that rigidified attitudes translate themselves into violence and an overstated need for assertions of masculinity in the home.

Maduro (1995) describes a parallel process within the Latino community. "We often experience. . . . being defined as a *machista* culture, as if male chauvinism were any lesser (rather than different) among Anglos. . . . we react at times by rejecting feminism as if it were just an Anglo issue, thus redoubling the frustration of Latinas' voices and struggles for their own specific liberation."

Similarly, any analysis of Asian or Muslim men must take into account their culture-specific definitions of masculinity and their intersection with dominant cultural prescriptions rather than simply superimposing the template of white privileged maleness.

Gay men operate largely outside hegemonic definitions of masculinity because, by virtue of their sexual orientation, they do not participate in the dominant culture's ethic of male sexual identity. They are perceived to be not truly men. The public violence of heterosexism and homophobia, which are both cross-cultural phenomena, creates and enforces notions of masculinity for all men that implicitly define maleness as anti-homosexual. Consistent with this stance is the tendency of what is masculine to be defined exclusively in opposition to what is considered feminine. Such constructions of masculinity predispose men to think of maleness as meaning domination in all its subtle or overt forms. Whether the context for the playing out of this domination is the military, the corporation, sports, pornography, or the family, societal norms for men encourage the devaluing of women, homosexuals, and men who are "other." These norms define social arrangements hierarchically and reinforce both rigid gender roles and the glorification of violence and oppression against both women and "other" men.

This brief overview of the specific ways that masculinity has been constructed and the ways those constructions often fail to take difference into account provides a point of departure for talking about the ways that therapy can become a context that permits the evolution of different constructions of maleness. Each of the respondents, Andres Nazario, a gay Latino therapist, William Doherty, a white heterosexual therapist, and Roberto Font, a gay Latino therapist, discuss their current formulations of maleness and go on to describe how they would intervene in the two following cases.

Each discussion is followed by a collective commentary by Claudia Bepko, a white lesbian, Rhea Almeida, a heterosexual woman from the Asian Indian diaspora (Uganda–third generation, first generation immigrant to this country), Yanella Stevenson, an African-Cuban lesbian, and

Theresa Messineo, a white heterosexual woman of mixed Italian and Austrian heritage.

The commentary responds to the revised version of each male contributors' discussion. Each was given the opportunity to respond to feedback by the women and re-write his piece. These revised versions are published here.

Case A

Lucas, an African American man in his thirties (both parents are from the South–they are teachers) is in a relationship with Shendi, also in her thirties, a woman of mixed racial heritage (her father is Irish and her mother is Chinese). Lucas is a young attorney who was just fired by his law firm because of what was described to him as an "attitude" problem. Shendi is a physician completing her residency in pediatrics. Her family is "reticent" about her relationship with Lucas because he is African American and because they are concerned that he cannot keep a job. Lucas' job loss is creating stress between him and Shendi. The stress is heightened because her family has been so covertly negative about their relationship.

Case B

Michael, an Irish man in his forties who is a graphics designer is in a semi-permanent relationship with Antonio, a computer programmer who is in his thirties. Michael is overweight. In contrast, Antonio is slim and attractive. The presenting problem involves continual fighting about their differences in body type and the differential access they experience in gay clubs. They describe their relationship as a committed one. However, Antonio frequents clubs where he has "recreational" sex and finds it difficult to understand why Michael is upset by this, since he thinks of himself as committed to the relationship. Michael explains that it is hurtful to him that the clubs Antonio goes to are places where Michael is not welcome. Because he is overweight, he is looked down on by the lean, muscular, "leather-wearing" men. Michael feels that if he is to be accepted, he must frequent S/M clubs or "bear" clubs where heavier, hairy men are acceptable.

ANDRES NAZARIO, JR.

The invitation to write about my "evolving construct of masculinity" has brought into focus how little I consider masculinity to be an important construct in my personal and professional life. Sociopolitical constructs such as nationality, race, gender, culture, sexual orientation, and socioeconomic status, to name a few, have often occupied much more space in my thinking than masculinity.

What does it mean to be male or female in this culture? What are the male privileges of a patriarchal system? What are the losses associated with being gay, Latino, or aging? I have pondered these and many other questions associated with the sociopolitical domains of existential meaning. But masculinity . . . does masculinity have to do with Charles Atlas, or with language?

Since concepts of "masculinity" begin to emerge at a very early age, I must revert back to thinking about masculinity, or other similar concepts, in my native language. In Spanish, *genero masculine* had to do much more with classification of words, such as those ending in "o," than with a construct of meaning. Words such as *hombré, varón,* and *macho* were probably more central constructs for me as I was growing up, and could perhaps translate into my English version of *masculinity.* The meanings I have attributed to these words are influenced by my family of origin, our cultural context within the larger culture of Cuba, and the social and political climate in the Island as I was growing up.

Macho (no appropriate English translation) refers to any male animal. My associations with the word macho (for humans) were primarily negative and oppressive, except as used in a few Mexican films I enjoyed as a kid. In those films, "machos" were actors like Jorge Negrete or Pedro Infante playing leading roles. They carried guns, sang popular corridos, and always ended up with the leading ladies. Otherwise, machos, from my perspective, were representatives of the oppressive and corrupted system of government and the military during the Batista dictatorship. Machos were aggressive, often abusive, brutal, and vulgar. They drank excessively and denigrated women.

Varón (male) refers to the qualities of being male such as strong, virile, sexual, aggressive, protective of women and children, often irresponsible, uncontrollable, and "mujeriego" (and therefore heterosexual). This is what I thought most boys aspired to be based on our cultural prescriptions.

Hombré (man) refers to the essence of being a man. Respectful and protective of women, self-absorbed, committed to one's principles, socially and politically motivated, willing to risk one's life for the well-being of others, committed to one's family, self-sacrificing, sexual. This is how I saw my father; this is what I aspired to be as I was growing up.

So if I were to assume that my constructs of masculinity derive from the internalization of my attributed meanings to the words *macho, varón,* and *hombré*, then my early constructs of masculinity have to do with the rejection of *macho*, the embracing of *hombré*, and curiosity about *varón*.

For an adolescent arriving in a foreign country as a political refugee, the constructs of survival, nationality, economics, and marginalization become more central. It is impossible to predict, but I am curious to question how my own constructs may or may not have changed given other circumstances or less traumatic events. Earning a living, learning a new language, adapting to a new culture, reconnecting with my parents in the USA, missing my grandparents and other extended family in Cuba, and other adaptations required of new immigrants took precedence.

Once I achieved a certain degree of acculturation, the meaning of sexual orientation and/or sexual preference became central in my life; once I became comfortable as a gay man, I lost my curiosity about *varón*, with the exception of its sexual component. Therefore, I dismissed some of my attributed qualities of masculinity, such as strong, virile, aggressive, irresponsible, often uncontrollable, and womanizer. Masculinity and heterosexuality somewhat appeared synonymous and, therefore, my construct of masculinity became even more marginalized. Being gay, then, meant more freedom to break away from prescribed roles. Given that at this time the sexual revolution and gay liberation were taking place, masculinity and gay pride for me were associated with sexual activity.

My early training as a family therapist was within a strategic model and, therefore, absent of issues related to gender. Once I became immersed in the feminist literature, I began to incorporate gender and other important domains into my work. Personally, I began to re-think my construct of *hombré*. Some of my attributed meanings became questionable. For example, I began to perceive how within the concept of respect for women, there was a belief in their fragility, or a "less-than-capable" assumption. I continue to have high regard and respect for women, but have attempted to free myself from the prescription of my culture that defined women as fragile and in subordinate positions. I now view masculinity, from an oppression-sensitive perspective, as within the domain of gender, influenced by other domains such as race, culture, socioeconomic status, ethnicity, sexual orientation, age, nationality, ability, and spirituality. These domains influence our perceptions and our realities, depending on our position vis-à-vis the dominant culture. Masculinity, I believe, cannot be isolated from these sociopolitical influences.

Case A

How do we know that they are heterosexuals? Just because they are married to each other? Or do we have additional information to confirm their heterosexuality? These issues should be part of the larger conversation.

Therapeutic Task

To engage in a conversation that will open space for the meanings attributed to their difficulties to emerge. This conversation will weave in issues of race, gender, socioeconomic status, nationality, ethnicity, careers, employment, spirituality/religion, culture, power, etc. The conversation should also open space for the struggle of young black males in this society to be part of the therapeutic dialogue. Some of the therapeutic questions I would like to ask as part of the conversation will be:

How did they decide to seek therapy to deal with this issue? How does Shendi define her primary concern? How does Lucas? Does he have an "attitude" problem or does society have an attitude toward his skin color? What difficulties has he encountered as a black male in demonstrating his competency? What has been Shendi's attitude about his loss of employment? What has Lucas' attitude been about her residency work? Which of their family members are more supportive of their struggles as a young professional couple? What has the impact on their relationship been of her parents' reticence about his race? Are both her parents equally reticent? Who else is reticent about his race? What reticence have each of them encountered relative to their race? What reticence does each have about the other? Does Shendi know how her parents may have overcome any reticence from others about their own relationship? What is society's attitude about their relationship? About his professional accomplishments? How is his attitude incongruent with that of other attorneys in his line of work? What attitude would liberate him from the present difficulty? What has been most helpful for them in the past in resolving conflicts? As a young black male, how has he been able to rebel against the dominant cultural prescription for black males?

This is the line of questions that I believe will illuminate the relationship between presenting problems and the couples' context. These also will lead to specific issues of gender and masculinity/femininity. Yet we must not assume that just because Lucas is black or Shendi is biracial that we know anything about them other than what is given in those few lines describing the case. How norms of masculinity/femininity collide or connect in their world needs to be part of the conversation. I prefer to be curious about these issues rather than to have preconceived definitions of their realities.

Case B

This case raises a lot of issues. Are these descriptions Michael's, Antonio's, or the therapist's? I would like to deconstruct, in dialogue with these clients, the following words and find their attributed meanings: overweight, semi-permanent, young, attractive, beautiful body, gay community, and S/M Clubs. Whose constructs are these? What impositions have these men accepted from each other? From the dominant culture? From the "gay culture?" These would be areas to explore:

What attracted them to each other? How did they negotiate the type of relationship they have? How have they resolved conflicts in the past? What visions do they have about how they would like their relationship to be? What are the issues associated with power in this relationship? What are the prescriptions for each of them from their families of origin? From their ethnic/cultural backgrounds? What would be the catastrophe if they were to unite against the subversive messages they are receiving? What impact does homophobia have in their lives? How do they defend themselves and their relationship from a heterosexist society? What impact do these issues have on the reasons that brought them to seek professional help?

As in the previous case, I would be curious about how they define their sense of gay pride and its possible connections to norms of sexuality/masculinity, without a preordained sense of what that should be for them.

The assumptions underlying the work with either of these couples would be based on an oppression-sensitive approach in which gender, race, ethnicity, culture, sexual orientation, spirituality, age, socioeconomic status, ability, nationality, and ecology are considered domains of existential meaning. These domains influence the manner in which our society operates and makes decisions. These domains also organize the therapeutic process in couples and family therapy. These sociopolitical domains influence the attitudes, perceptions, and behaviors of clients, therapists, supervisors, institutions, and other larger systems. They are always connected with presenting problems.

In addition, I must share my discomfort with the focus on masculinity that has taken place over the last ten years or so. My views on Robert Bly, John Bradshaw, and men's drumming are not very positive. I saw this emphasis on men's issues as an attempt by the patriarchal (heterosexual) system to regain any ground lost to the women's movement. Therefore, I connect the emphasis on masculinity and men's issues with the attempts of conservative, white, heterosexual males to maintain power. I am willing to critically challenge my views on this issue.

RESPONSES TO ANDRES NAZARIO

You present an in-depth analysis of masculinity from two different vantage points and you contextualize masculinity in its differing social expressions. Considerations about being male or female. . . . male privileges in a patriarchal system . . . losses associated with being gay . . . are all connected to definitions of masculinity: Your freedom to break away from prescribed norms is in fact not separate from masculinity, but perhaps an expression of role flexibility. Therefore, the positive aspects of gay manhood could in fact expand narrow prescriptions of heterosexual manhood. You suggest in response to our question if "commitment may imply different things to them" that there are no norms applicable to gay couples, yet the literature and our clinical experience suggests otherwise (Laird & Green, 1996). How do you offer heterosexual men positive "select narratives" from the dominant prescriptions? Your opening discourse about whether or not we know if Lucas and Shendi are heterosexual is great. You did not accept the definitions assumed in the case description, or the descriptions offered by the couple themselves, but instead would ask the couple to examine their biases with respect to couplehood and heterosexuality. What are some of your opening questions to invite such dialogue?

You do a wonderful job of integrating questions that embrace the societal, intergenerational, and interpersonal levels of the problem. Of particular interest is the way that you needed to sort out the importance of issues in your own life and the order in which you did that: first racial and cultural issues because they were a matter of survival, then issues of sexuality and sexual orientation. Issues of masculinity and gender were the last to be dealt with. You indicate that your sense of masculinity took a back seat to problems of acculturation. As sexual preference became a focus and you became "comfortable as a gay man," what construct of masculinity did you either incorporate or reject? If masculinity and heterosexuality were synonymous for you, what did being a gay man mean to you? How did sexual orientation change your sense of masculinity? Are there any aspects of macho, varón, and hombré that can be deconstructed to provide new meanings and form?

Issues of gender are important ones for you to explore further, because without a more in-depth analysis of it, men sometimes fail to recognize the privilege inherent in being a man, even if they are gay men.

In terms of your responses to case A, a problem is that we don't really know from the case description what the couple is looking for in coming for therapy. The "problem" has not really been defined here. But we would want to know much more about how Lucas perceives the problem and whether he has any consciousness of the impact of his race. What sense does he get of what people define as an appropriate "attitude" in the work environment and does he feel it's influenced by their "attitudes" about race? How does he perceive power relationships–both in the workplace and in his marriage/family?

You address directly what Shendi's experiences of racism and heterosexism might be, and suggest that her perceptions of masculinity are important to the understanding of the problems in this case.

Do you think it is important to ask Lucas and Shendi questions about their sexuality and cultural tradtions as well as their relationship to pornography? You question how norms of masculinity/femininity collide or connect in this couple's world. You did not ask any questions regarding Lucas's family of origin, their view on this relationship, his view about his father or other men in his life and their definitions of masculinity–did you omit this for a specific reason?

In Case B, you begin with a deconstruction of the couples' language. Your question, "What are the issues associated with power in this relationship?" is an important one to explore further. It is important not to assume equality in gay relationships simply because the two people involved are of the same sex. Case B brings together a multitude of issues therapists would need to attend to–how does the larger context of heterosexim, power and privilege enter into the lives of Michael and Antonio in ways that entrap their intimate life? What are the critical issues to be raised in teaching largely heterosexual therapists? What are the dimensions of power that are obscured because it is a gay couple?

It would be important to deconstruct the couple's ideas of commitment. Commitment may mean something very different to them than it does to, say, heterosexual couples. Gay men frequently have very different norms about monogamy and recreational sex. What does the term "semi-permanent" in the case description mean? Michael, in this description, feels shamed and somewhat one down because Antonio goes to clubs to have sex with men who are not like him. Is Antonio implicitly saying that he finds Michael unattractive? Has he been overly influenced by the stereotypes of masculinity in the gay community that favor lean, hard-bodied men to heavier, hairier ones? What about the power differential in the relationship that leaves Michael in a state of feeling excluded and to some degree marginalized by his own lover?

One might question, "How does being white give Michael power because Antonio is Latino?" Or, "How does having a beautiful body give Antonio power because Michael is older and overweight?" What work has Michael done to understand his own racism? Does Antonio feel Michael understands his race and culture? Would Antonio be less likely to go to clubs for sex if Michael were more sensitive to the racism?

How would you assess their links to the gay community? Would you refer them to a gay pride center, a group for addressing various differences in gay couples or to NOMAS?

Regarding Robert Bly, we are very much in agreement. It was heartening to see you comment on the subset of the men's movement that has not been helpful to men. We had hoped you would elaborate on particulars of this movement that are destructive to women and families.

WILLIAM DOHERTY

I am writing during the criminal trials of a number of military men who have been accused of sexually harassing and raping women under their command. This national discussion about women in the military, and of men's attitudes and behavior toward women in the military, focuses public attention like nothing else on the idea of masculinity. Indeed, war has been the quintessential province of men, the defining difference between the sexes. Men kill; women give and nurture life. Although women have gained a place in the military in many countries of the world, nowhere are they permitted to do combat duty on the ground. Being a combat soldier has been to masculinity what being a midwife has been to women: it is clearly something only men can do adequately.

Although only a relatively small minority of men enter the military nowadays, every boy knows he might have to go to war someday. And many societies worry about whether their young men will be up to the task if called. Like many other men, I struggle with two competing perspectives on the military and masculinity. The first is that soldiering reflects the dark side of masculinity, the propensity of men to dominate others, to hold onto power by whatever means necessary. The military embodies fear and loathing of homosexuals and of women who would assert their power, and it has a checkered history in dealing with soldiers of color who see the military as an option for a better life.

From this first perspective, the military culture of masculinity poisons the rest of the culture. Our male heroes are often military men; witness the massive support for Colin Powell when he considered a presidential bid. The next highest category of male heroes are action/adventure movie stars, men playing roles of cool risk-taking and effortless destruction. In this culture of masculinity, being a man is defined as having power over others, especially over women. And the military power structure becomes the ultimate symbol of a powerful nation that can have its way with other nations.

As appealing and straightforward as this "toxic masculinity" perspective is for understanding what ails the military and the male gender, focusing only on the dark side of masculinity leads to polarization within individual men's consciousness and within the culture at large. It represents a deficit model of masculinity that leads to defensiveness among most men and self-loathing among a few. (A male classmate of my daughter's summed up a discussion of masculinity with the phrase: "Men are scum.")

From the second perspective, soldiering, like other aspects of masculine culture, is informed by a positive ideal, albeit one that is easily distorted. In the case of the military, the core ideal is that of protecting one's family and community, even at the risk of losing one's life. Additional ideals revolve around honor, duty, and loyalty. Indeed, military service has helped many young men learn to be responsible in their behavior. Not many of us would dispute the importance of military service during World War II when true forces of evil threatened the world (although, of course, that war itself was brought on partly by stupid imperialistic wars of the past). In military culture at its best, protecting one's country is the motivating force, and the use of brute power the sometimes necessary means. The challenge that sexual harassment illuminates is the tendency of the military ideal to become corrupted into a stance where domination and intimidation become elevated over the ideals of protection, honor, and duty.

My evolving approach as a clinician and member of the wider culture is to stress the potential linkages between aspects of traditional masculinity and the new social environment in which men find themselves. Being an honorable man now involves accepting and even promoting partnership with women in all aspects of life, including the military. The mature man does not reject or disdain the protector role; rather, he sees it as mostly involved with the same kind of buffering nurturance and support that women offer to their loved ones. And he is not threatened by the sexual orientation of other men and women.

Only occasionally does the contemporary civilian man need to protect his loved ones from physical harm, but I believe that a readiness to do so is a core and valued part of most men's psychology and should not be devalued. I recall the time I defended my wife from a lurching drunk on a New York subway. I used enough force to move him back to a seat. I had no desire to harm him, but I knew I would go as far as I needed to go to protect my wife from him. When there are strange noises in the basement of the house, there is nothing patriarchal about the man going down there first to check for intruders.

Connecting traditional masculine virtues, such as courage, honor, duty, and self-sacrifice, and men's new responsibilities to share power and respect women as equal partners is my strategy in therapy and in teaching. In the broader public arena, the military might become a crucible for transforming the culture of masculinity in our time.

Case A

The problem I have with discussing Couple A is that the presenting relationship issue is not apparent. The vignette describes two problems: Lucas' being fired from his job and Shendi's family being reticent about her relationship with an African-American man and about his job prospects. I will assume that those are the two problems that brought the couple into therapy.

Lucas brings into the relationship the dual issues of being African-American and being a man. On the ethnicity side, although Shendi is from a biracial family, being half Chinese and half Irish does not lead to the same level of stigmatization in American society as does being African-American. And both Irish and Chinese peoples, although having their own histories of discrimination in coming to America, often focus on their distance from African-Americans in terms of social status. Shendi is likely to have internalized these beliefs and attitudes.

Add the masculinity issue to the picture and you have a double whammy. Even though Lucas has gone to law school, he must generate employment income on a consistent basis in order to be seen as a responsible man by Shendi's family, and perhaps also by Shendi and Lucas himself. A man who "can't hold a job" is seen as not being a real man in our society. And African-American men have been given the stereotype of particularly poorly suited for success in the workforce: either they are unemployed and unmotivated, underemployed through lack of skills or initiative, or they received their well-paid job through affirmative-action quotas. Any way they turn, their ability to provide for their families is suspect, particularly when they lose a job.

I would approach these issues through an exploration of Shendi's and Lucas' beliefs about masculinity and race. I would probably start with Shendi's family of origin: What do they say about Lucas and the couple's relationship? What concerns do they express about Lucas' job prospects? Then I would move into Shendi's own beliefs and the origins of these beliefs, and then to Lucas'. I would then want to explore what happened with Lucas at the job, to explore how masculinity and race might have affected his work experience. As a European-American therapist, I would have to be particularly focused on learning from Lucas about his experience and perceptions, while still being willing to offer questions and challenges.

Because both spouses have probably had considerable conversations about the role of race in their relationship, I would imagine that the newer material for them would be masculinity and its intersection with race. In exposing and critiquing the traditional expectations of masculinity, I would be careful not to treat the provider role from a deficit perspective, or to make the assumption that African-American men don't value the provider role as much as other men. Where I would go specifically with them would depend on where this initial exploration leads.

Case B

As a straight man with limited clinical experience with the issue that Antonio and Michael are facing, I would spend considerable time learning about their perspectives and feelings. I would want to know what it meant to Antonio to keep the option of gay bars in his life. How does this fit into his self-image and his sense of his individual needs? How does it define the relationship with Michael? How does Michael respond to Antonio's concerns and complaints: with compassion, rational arguments, disdain, distancing, or other ways? If Antonio says he can't live with Michael's lifestyle, is Michael willing to give up his relationship with Antonio over this issue?

For Antonio, I would want to explore the same kinds of issues from his perspective, in addition to trying to understand how his self-image is threatened by Michael's greater perceived attractiveness. How much is Antonio's issue about outside sex and how much about invidious comparison about attractiveness? If more the latter, I would explore how he lets the evaluations of strangers determine his feelings about himself and his partner.

In addition to these explorations from a stance of "not knowing," I would bring a value stance related to mainstream cultural images of masculinity. That is, I am struck with how it seems easier for men in relationships (with men or women) to justify pursuing their individual needs despite the cost to the other person and the relationship. I think of a husband who insisted on going hunting most of the fall weekends despite his wife's plea that she was overburdened with a job all week and solo child care on the weekends he was gone. This husband simply felt entitled: A man has to do what a man has to do. I wonder if this kind of male entitlement plays a role in Michael and Antonio's relationship; namely, that Antonio feels entitled to outside sexual relationships no matter how threatening they are to his partner. If this seems to be the case, I would explore the moral equation in their relationship between commitment to self and commitment to the well-being of the other and the partnership, and what this equation says about Michael and Antonio as men who care for each other.

RESPONSES TO BILL DOHERTY

Bill Doherty: "War has been the quintessential province of men–the defining difference between the sexes."

Elevating the structure of the military in a feminist journal is somewhat a contradiction. Your comment: "men kill, women give and nurture life," is a social construction–not a state of nature–so using this as a starting point for talking about liberating forms of masculinity underscores many of the already-critiqued dilemmas around the obfuscation of gender and power. Men have constructed war as a function of their will to dominate. Is aggression an inherently male trait? This smacks of essentialism. There are very many aggressive women, and many gentle men. Ghandi was, after all, a man.

You equate aggression, territoriality, cruelty, with maleness when in fact it is the case that men have been socialized to *show* these traits. You say, "Being a combat soldier has been to masculinity what being a mid-wife has been to women." But men have been delivering babies for generations–they robbed women of the midwife role for economic gain and domination. It is doubtful that most of the men who managed to return from Vietnam see their participation in that war as a positive expression of their masculinity.

Defining men's military roles as honorable obscures their more destructive dimensions–namely, that the structure of the military and war is socially constructed and is oppressive to other men, women and children. This seems obvious in the case of the Germans and the Holocaust, the right-wing Israelis and their exile from a Palestinian homeland, the fundamentalist Arab nations' killing of young boys and women under the guise of fighting the anti-Muslim sentiment of the West, the anti-colonialist military takeover of the Asian Pacific, as well as US imperialism worldwide. All of these military systems participate in the large scale domination of human life. It is common knowledge that the socialization of men in the military involves the cutting off of emotionality and the degradation of women and family in order to create excellent "combat" soldiers. What about the fact that in Desert Storm men and women of color were disproportionately represented in dangerous missions? Their entry into the military is directly linked to deindustrialization here and the global expansion of Corporate America that contributed to the large scale unemployment of men and women of color who were over-represented in blue collar jobs. What does it mean for the masculinity of African American men that while they are jobless and invisible at home they are celebrated for giving up their lives in the military and protecting white America?

Your analysis, which deems service in the military to be an honorable experience for men, obscures the larger implication of such a value system, as well as the racist and homophobic biases that have been a pervasive part of military life.

In our opinion, the military can never become a crucible for transforming the culture of masculinity because its very premise is one of domination. It is not courageous or honorable to kill. The larger question is: can men be heroes without the sword? Without destruction? What would that courage look like?

Your definition of masculinity was surprising in its essential self-focus. You define masculinity exclusively within the context of personal experience and as a clinician there is always the responsibility to make one's personal experience relevant to the larger socio-political context. The concept of seeing men as protectors has many implications, one of which might be to justify world violence, domestic violence, and other forms of domination, power and control—all in the guise of protection.

In response to your "intruder" scenario for instance, some of us are lesbian. What do we call it when either our partner or one or both of us goes downstairs to check for an intruder? Matriarchal? Do we ascribe too much maleness to the one of us wielding the baseball bat? Do we bemoan the fact that there's no male in the house? (besides the intruder)—and stay cowering in our bed? You elevate the role of the male as protector, but it *is* in fact a patriarchal construction to assume that someone weak needs someone strong and the strong one is always male and the weak one is always female.

In his book *Refusing to Be a Man*, John Stoltenberg (1989) quotes Virginia Woolf on her feelings about men and war:

> Therefore if you insist upon fighting to protect me or 'our' country, let it be understood, soberly and rationally between us, that you are fighting to gratify a sex instinct which I cannot share, to procure benefits which I have not shared and probably will not share; but not to gratify my instincts or to protect myself or my country. For . . . in fact, as a woman, I have no country.

> –Virginia Woolf, *Three Guineas*

The very concept of preservation of the traditional male role raises many troubling issues, even in the guise of "honor" and "duty to country." What we see in the backlash against feminism is that the idea of promoting partnership with women in all aspects of life including the military is quite frightening. The tradition of the military has been and continues to be abusive to women. Domestic violence is rampant in the experience of military wives. Women and children in the military are quite isolated and suffer greatly from moving from place to place, having no roots. The notion of respecting the tradition of male honor and duty is analogous to sanctioning the historic position of men as dominating women in all aspects of home and community life. Currently, women who work outside the home are held responsible for the ills of their children and homes. The disadvantages and inequity to women and children of the traditional male role in families are never part of this discourse. The voices of women and children whose male partners/fathers are incarcerated as part of this country's fastest growing "home" industry are entirely silenced.

Defensiveness and self-loathing among men *are* problems that need to be reckoned with. However the conceptual error in your argument lies in the assumption that if men do not embrace at least a part of what they have been taught by their traditional male socialization (i.e., "protection" of women, children and country by force and violence), that defensiveness and self-loathing are inevitable. However, if men developed a broader, more relationally protective perspective on masculinity that valued negotiation, compromise, and rational debate more than brute force, their self-loathing would become unnecessary. We need to replace a "power over" with a "power with" discourse.

Though space limitations might have prevented this, it might have been more relevant to discuss your formulation of the ways your class, race, gender, economic and professional status help you to construct your own sense of masculinity.

You pose many interesting questions in the first case. Nevertheless, many others were missing. How were the families of this couple situated in relation to their being a couple? Were each of the families in agreement with this union? Where did Lucas' parents teach—in public school, a university? What were their perceptions of "attitudinal problems" in their son? What were their feelings about their son's cross-cultural relationship? How did Lucas perceive himself on the job? How does he define himself?

We do agree with your analysis of the ways that racism may be impacting Lucas and Shendi. However, you are not clear about how you would bridge issues of race and gender. It is unclear what you mean when you say you "would be careful not to treat Lucas' provider role from a deficit perspective." What is the alternative? The bombardment of racial attacks that African American men experience often leads to a rigidifying of their need to provide and protect and this rigidity may result in a devaluing and subordination of women's roles as a result. Lucas is experiencing the impact of both racism (his access to the provider role is thwarted) and sexism (the family expects him to be a good provider because he is the male). To not view Lucas' ability to provide from a deficit perspective would be to broaden his perspective of what it might mean to him to be a provider in the context of a collaborative relationship with a woman.

In the second case, what is glaring is your lack of knowledge about gays and lesbians juxtaposed as it is with your knowledge of and comfort with the military. It is positive that you would spend time learning from them about the issues that Michael and Antonio are facing, however, one would hope that you would also spend time reading and consulting with other therapists. It is unclear what "issues" you are referring to having limited clinical experience with–gay issues? Issues of domination in sexual relationships? Cultural issues? Body objectification issues? Your question for Michael–"How much does he let the evaluation of strangers determine his feelings about himself and his partner?"–places too much emphasis on Michael's intrapsychic process and too little emphasis on socialization, sexism and homophobia. The question implies that Michael should not allow strangers to determine his attractiveness without an analysis of this tendency as a universal process with particular implications for gay men of color in interracial relationships. A different question that takes the emphasis off Michael might be: What messages from society dictate who is attractive and who is not? Who is most susceptible to these messages and why? What does one's race, gender and sexual orientation have to do with one's level of susceptibility to these messages?

The focus on male entitlement is a good one. However, again, it would be important to explore how male entitlement played out differently in this particular couple. What gives one man greater entitlement over another man? What other types of entitlement (or lack thereof) do the men in this couple experience? Entitlement due to race? To social class? Lack of entitlement due to sexual orientation? For example, does Antonio's lack of entitlement due to his race and sexual orientation make him more or less likely to be polygamous? How does this couple think about issues of sex outside the relationship? Do they feel more entitled to recreational sex because of messages about sexuality and commitment in the gay community? It is important in exploring this theme not to restrict questions to ones that are more applicable to white, heterosexual couples. You impose some moral judgments on the couple that may not be consistent with ideas about sexuality and commitment among gay men.

ROBERTO FONT

CUBAN-ITALIAN, 23
5'9" M 160#, straight looking and acting, athletic, lean. Seeking a Latino with a brain for friendship, hanging out, movies, music and conversation. Must be masculine, good looking and athletic, 28 and younger, no fats, no femmes or drugs (Hx-7-22).

ASIAN DREAM WANTS EUROBOY
Boyish Asian-American with a boyish body, 29, 5'8", healthy, friendly, well educated. Want to meet a lean, smooth, good looking, versatile, HIV − European, 18-30 (Hx-7-22).

SUBMISSION AS AN ART FORM
Sensual, romantic, successful, dominant businessman, 37, ISO (in search of) confident, imaginative, submissive woman. (*Village Voice*, 10-7-97).

Given the complexity of gender cross-culturally, I will attempt to provide some thoughts that I have been struggling with regarding issues of masculinity and clinical practice. As a gay man, as a Latino, and as an immigrant, my own marginalization has freed me to explore multiple ways of being a man. While gay culture has a particular advantage in understanding oppression from margin to center, not all gay men maintain this openness. Contrary to common assumption, not all gay men are warm, sensitive, and nonsexist. Gay men of all races have been socialized in a heterosexual context, and cannot totally escape sexism. White gay men have access to white heterosexual male privilege through passing, and are at risk of misusing that privilege. Gay men of color have access to male privilege. Misogyny exists in gay male communities.

Masculinity is both an image and a set of behaviors that boys are socialized, from birth, to believe constitute maleness. As we explore the meaning of male ideals of masculine image and behavior, it is vital to remember two things. First, these constructions are contextual, meaning that they vary from culture to culture, and are impacted by racism, heterosexism, classism, and cultural form. The second thing to keep in mind is that the one commonality among all cultural constructs of masculinity is that they are defined by the patriarchy, which means that men are always defining for themselves what masculinity is. This is a significant departure from the construction of femininity, because women do not have the power to define for themselves what femininity looks like and how a feminine woman should behave. It continues to be a male privilege to create and perpetuate those definitions in most cultures. But simply because masculinity is male-defined does not mean it is a "true" or even desirable definition for most of the male population. The inherent problem with a patriarchal definition of masculinity is that it privileges a certain body type, sexual orientation, class, race, and ethnic type of man. Not all men are treated equally. Domination and subordination are the mechanisms of patriarchy, oppressing women as well as men who are racially or sexually different from the norm. The ideals of masculinity from which men operate under the patriarchy are severely limiting and ought to be questioned and challenged.

What Is a Man Supposed to Look Like?

The physical ideals of masculinity are centered on the question of what a man ought to look like. These ideals have changed and shifted in each generation. George Washington wore a powdered wig and was considered a manly man; Louis XIV wore make-up and frilly clothing and set the fashion for much of European manhood; men in the post-war United States wore a uniform of short hair, suit and tie. The ideal masculine look also varies depending on culture: in segments of gay male culture, large muscles, boyishness, and hairless bodies are now considered the ideal of masculinity. In many Latin American countries, men with mustaches are considered masculine-looking because facial hair signifies a rite of passage.

Gay men of all races are faced with a unique dilemma: by virtue of being gay, they are already dismissed as failing to be truly masculine, because the patriarchal definition of masculinity is predicated on heterosexuality. Segments of the gay male community have objectified an image of masculinity that is class-based; for example, construction workers, lumberjacks, cowboys, and uniformed men, uniforms depicting a sense of institutional power (Rofes, 1997). Likewise, wanting to be straight-acting, or valuing other men who are straight-acting, is a common thread of gay male culture. Not surprisingly, because of heterosexism, gay male ideals of masculinity are constructed in relationship to narrow constructs of heterosexism. Personal advertisements in gay papers commonly reflect such themes. This is both internalized homophobia and heterosexism, a collusion with the patriarchal definition of masculinity.

The physical ideals of masculinity are embedded in a cultural context and are constructed through gender role socialization. These are influenced through the roles in the family and social structures such as the media. Pornography is a particularly powerful transmitter of messages about masculinity. In gay cultures, pornography has played a large role in defining gay masculinity and gay ideals of male beauty. For both straight and gay men, penis size has become an obsessive and compartmentalized measure of masculinity. While there are some significant differences around gender development, for gay men what gets punctuated repeatedly are the dominant norms of patriarchy.

How Does a Real Man Act?

The second construct of masculinity involves the development of male norms that are deeply embedded in sexism. For example, there are gay men who have adopted a more feminine stance but become self-critical to the point of referring to themselves as "slut." This is another example of devaluing female qualities even within gay communities. Masculine norms, even within the gay community, are often developed in contrast to feminine norms as defined by the patriarchy. The two are seen as opposites. By having markedly separate physical presentations and codes of behavior, men differentiate themselves from women. This is a vital part of the social construction of masculinity in Western culture: the worst insult a man can give to another man is to call him a "pussy" or any other epithet that compares him to a female. The usual norms of masculinity involve avoiding anything that is feminine (i.e., housework, nurturing children, being relational and emotive). The masculine norm includes being overtly homophobic–the second worst thing a man can call another man is "fag."

In gay male sexuality, some of the constructs of masculinity play out in terms of who is the top (dominant, penetrator) and who is the bottom (passive, being penetrated) during sex. As we explore the construction of masculinities, we have to wonder how that framework for thinking about gender roles and sexual positions evolved. Was it more dichotomous a few decades ago, and is it now moving toward more versatility? How much of it is the construction of masculinity, and how much of it is a carryover of domination/subordination themes of heterosexism?

What Happens to Men Who Don't Fit the Masculine Mold?

In gay culture, the ideals of masculine beauty, such as youth and muscularity, slenderness, and a smooth body elude many men who struggle with self-esteem, because they can never achieve the ideal. This is similar to the ways women struggle against ideal constructions of womanhood.

Gay men respond to these experiences of oppression through clinical manifestations of eating disorders, substance abuse, and other mental-health difficulties. Another parallel to women's struggle is that of aging; older gay men are often referred to as "trolls" by younger gay men. These social pressures are some of the hidden dimensions of gay men's masculinities that seriously impact their mental health.

One solution to countering this body-beautiful ideal is the development of alternative social groups. Different ideals in body types are represented in "bear" clubs or Girth and Mirth social clubs where large and/or hairy men are valued and pursued by each other and also by those who do not fit the profile, frequently called "twinkies." In New York City, bears have found a space in S/M and leather clubs. Some bears participate in the S/M scene; others do not. These clubs provide more acceptance than the "Chelsea-boy crowd" clubs (smooth and well-muscled young gay men). By elevating hairiness and largeness, gay men may be creating a new norm. The very notion of using clubs as a self-enhancing context may need to be challenged.

As it is for women, the problem for so many men–gay, bisexual, trans-gendered, and heterosexual–is objectification. The patriarchy teaches us to value the exterior appearance far more than the inner being of each individual. Men are taught that their sexuality responds to visual stimulation, from which a culture is born.

What Are the Positive Aspects of Masculinity?

The construction of masculinities is constantly evolving, but the one common link, historically, is that it has always been defined by men. We need to begin to look at the positive aspects of masculinity. What are they? How can we construct new norms that are respectful of women, people of color, and people who are considered "other" in society?

For many men of color, there are multiple and complex factors that feed into the construction of masculinity. For example, there is the need to adapt to racist culture, often to take care of siblings and sometimes to be translators for parents. These challenging experiences have positive aspects for men in particular. Fostering a sense of connectedness to family and community early on in a boy's life is a critical factor. Some of the overtly positive constructions of masculinity in Latino culture include the ideal of being a man of your word, which may mean many things, including being honest, sincere, and having respect, giving and receiving, but especially giving respect. There is also the ideal of men being loving and warm and caring to their children and partners. Many of these values, however, collide with a negative definition of masculinity. For example, being a man of your word runs counter to proving your manhood by sleeping with as many women as possible; being a loving and respectful partner contradicts responding to any woman who offers to have sex with you; a man who does not respond to sexual overtures runs the risk of being labeled a *maricon* (faggot)! The cross-cultural proscription of men's physicality and normative patterns vary.

Along with the way men act out traditional norms, they also conduct themselves in particular ways that involve voice, tone, gestures. For example, "... a South Asian man is likely to have a sensibility that incorporates more of the 'feminine' than his Western counterpart"; "unfortunately, this does not necessarily change his view of gender roles" (Ratti, 1993, p. 49). In white American culture, a mincing walk and flamboyant gestures throw a man's sexual orientation into question. Likewise, expressions of emotion, such as crying, which are seen as feminine, are rejected as being part of the masculine ideal. Men are supposed to be strong and commanding, sure of themselves, and athletic. This is the ideal of masculinity that boys are taught to admire and emulate in mainstream U.S. culture. However, in many Latin American countries, crying is acceptable in certain contexts, such as the death of a family member. Boyd-Franklin (1989) describes role flexibility in black families. One example of this dynamic occurs when the oldest child, whether male or female, is placed in a parental role as nurturer, or caretaker of his siblings. Although connected to a history of poverty and economic hardship, this dynamic is helpful in expanding the role of young boys.

Case A

As family-systems therapists who are working from a her/historical stance of relationship, we are always curious about the development of an individual/familial and social context as it pertains to the presenting problem. I offer this ethical curiosity as a rationale for inquiring about "seemingly unrelated" information or I will encourage the clients to offer some of their own constructions around the presenting institution of marriage/relationship/racial identity and intimacy as it embraces heterosexism/homophobia and therapy organizes the couple's relationships. Along these lines, it is also important to know the type and extent of community support that is available to couples. For example, some questions that would be asked are as follows: What social supports do they have in the community church, civic organizations, etc.? To understand the family's consciousness around race, the following questions might be helpful: Who in his family has chosen to marry outside of their race? What was the family's reaction to this? Who embraced or supported the couple's decision? Who didn't? How was this different or similar to his choice to marry a biracial woman? Has he ever been in an interracial relationship? If so, how did he negotiate family and community responses? What experiences has he had with members of his racial community? If there has been pressure, how has he dealt with it? What is his understanding of the pressure? Questions to Shendi would include her understanding of her parents' and her family's response, and her connection to the Chinese/Irish racial/cultural identity.

In attempting to unwrap some of the distinctions around dimensions of power and control within the relationship, I would first elicit from Lucas his views on how men's and women's lives are shaped within the locus of the family. After engaging Lucas in a conversation about society's views of men, and black men in particular, I would be interested in furthering this conversation around themes of loss. Acknowledgment of loss with respect to masculinity expands experiences of emotional vulnerability. Loss within the African-American community is of particular significance with respect to ideas of masculinity. For example, I would ask questions like: What are acceptable ways to express loss for men in general and men in his racial community? What have been his historical and immediate losses in his family and among friends? What is his experience of job loss? How does this relate to his status as a man, an African-American man, and his relationship with the culture's limited access to economic opportunity? A discussion of this nature sets the stage for connecting Lucas' experience to men as a class, and focuses less on his personal constructions of manhood. Dialogues of this nature serve both to heighten a man's awareness of male socialization and provide a language for differentiating personal choices from those institutionally created. Expanding the conversation of masculinity as it pertains to his relationship difficulties offers new visions of courage that are often shut down through daily discourse and interaction with public life. As it relates to the interior of his relationship, I would ask for specific ways in which he participates in the areas of emotional relatedness, physical contact and intimacy, and all of the second-shift responsibilities. What is their thinking as a couple about money, plans for children, and child-rearing. For example: Who initiates sex? How would they describe their sex life? Is pornography used as part of their sexual life? If so, how? How has pornography impacted and shaped his sexuality and understanding of intimacy? Sexuality in all of its complex forms is critical to understanding aspects of the structure of intimacy.

The whole topic of S/M is a controversial one in heterosexual, homosexual, and bisexual communities. Probably due to marginalization of sexual orientations other than heterosexuality, S/M may appear more visible in gay and lesbian communities. Within the gay, lesbian, and bisexual communities, this issue is controversial due to homophobia and internalized homophobia. The issue of S/M may not be addressed or questioned in public spheres out of a gay person's fear of being further marginalized. The fact is that S/M cuts across sexual orientations and a therapist needs to attend to the issues as they relate to the couple, regardless of the couple's or therapist's sexual orientation. The dynamics of domination and subordination in sex acts and the power dynamic across gender, race, and economic lines are bound to impact the couple's relationship.

Couples often have a difficult time describing gendered patterns within the interior of their relationship, their families and in the culture in general. Therefore, I might utilize a number of edits from common films to highlight issues of gender, race, culture, class and sexual orientation. (These ideas are integrated from the *Cultural Context Model*; Almeida et al., 1998.) Illustrations of films are used to deconstruct the intersectionality of gender, race, culture, class, and sexual orientation. Conversations include how both heterosexism and homophobia impact and control the choices men make in public and family life. This dialogue allows men to see how their masculinity, especially the negative aspects, is also shaped by these rigid constructions. For example, I would ask Lucas how his expression of nurturance toward his partner or involvement with traditionally female household tasks in the presence of his male friends influences his choice to be respectful of his partner? These themes are used for all couples to provide context that counters the emotional and social segregation so central to our culture.

Case B

Similar to the process of preparing the context that I articulated in the previous case, I would set the stage for inquiring about the range of issues surrounding the socialization of gender with gay couples. Understanding the socialization context provides the therapist and the couple a better sense of the power dynamics in the relationship, along with helping to gain an understanding of the ways heterosexism/homophobia play out within their families and in public institutions that they encounter daily.

In assessing the power dynamics of this couple, I would want to get a reading of how their lives are situated in three major contexts: the larger culture, the familial context, and the interior/interpersonal context. For example, Michael and Antonio would be asked to identify the forms of public violence they have experienced because of their sexual orientation. I would want them to have a conversation about how this impacts their relationship. Antonio would be asked to talk about race-based violence.

Do they get support from each other around these issues? ₁ ways? This would provide a context of joining with the coup₁ acknowledgment of a collective experience for gays and les articulating the distinctions across gender, race, and culture.

I would then want to understand something about their fami₁ experiences as they relate to male/female norms and homosexuality. For example, some questions may include: Who in your respective families knows about your orientation? Who is supportive? Who is not? Do they honor your relationship in the same way as your heterosexual siblings? If parents have knowledge of the relationship, what concerns, if any, do they have about the couple being interracial?

Finally, I would assess their understanding of the presenting problem in relationship to categories of emotional relatedness and commitment. For example, some questions would be asked about the history of the relationship: What is Michael and Antonio's definition of "committed to each other"? At what point did they define themselves as a couple? I would explore what this couple defines as "continuous fighting." To address some of the body image and sexuality issues presented by the couple, it is important to track the couple's process of defining couplehood as it relates to norms of sexuality within the gay community.

While there would be space to address Antonio's seemingly assaultive behavior toward Michael, I would be very careful not to privilege Michael's initial description of his marginalization. Expanding the context and situating the couple's total experience is critical to not joining with Michael over what appears to be a deep pain. What appears to be Antonio's lack of integrity is often a response to multiple experiences of social and interpersonal assault on one's sense of being, both in the public and the private domains. Within this particular relationship, it would be important to elicit whether he is controlled economically, racially, educationally, etc. Antonio's decision to engage in certain sexual activities may involve particulars of the relationship and gender role socialization. For example, it is this therapist's experience that with many older white gay men, who are often victimized and even battered, there is a history of economic and racial exploitation toward younger gay men.

One of the tasks in therapy is assessing sexuality along a continuum of gender role socialization within gay men's experience. Gay men have received too many messages about their sexuality that have been detrimental to self. By connecting men across sexual orientation, it allows gay men to confront negative aspects of masculinity while maintaining gay pride and embracing positive constructions of masculinity. Some examples of positive constructions of masculinity include the successful integration of positive female norms. Some examples are, emotional availability and relatedness, collaboratively sharing the provider role and not privileging it as an indicator of manhood, redefining intimacy and sexuality (moving away from objectification), and resisting rigid norms. Many of these positive constructions of masculinity are explored in this paper.

The evolution of new constructions of masculinity in both cases starts with the initiation of dismantling existing constructs of masculinities. Although the questions and conversations mentioned in this article can be elicited in a couples' or individual session, it is this therapist's experience that a "profeminist men's group" is the most powerful context within which to embrace new expressions of masculinity. The group, as a collective community, provides an opportunity for resocialization experiences with built-in support that bridges therapy to community life. The paradigm for addressing the new forms of masculinity has to be one that is larger than the unit of couple or family system.

RESPONSES TO ROBERTO FONT

It was reassuring to see you define the significant categories that organize intimate partnering, with each category existing along a continuum between all couples:

1. emotional connection to emotional isolation,
2. physical affection to physical abuse,
3. shared economic responsibility to misuse/abuse of economic power,
4. shared parenting, under responsibility, psychological neglect to abusive parenting,
5. sexual intimacy to sexual abuse with pornography, S/M and the knowing transmission of HIV,
6. immigration as a positive influence to the use of this status to wield power in all or some of the above categories,
7. from positive contributions of male/race privilege to misuse/abuse of male and race privilege in the form of job relocation, language barriers, economic dependence, etc.
8. communicating respectfully to use of intimidation with one's partner in the form of gestures, actions, loud voices, destroying property and driving the car at excessive speed.

But having outlined all of these categories, you then choose to illustrate actual questioning in the one area that therapists have the most difficulty addressing, namely sexuality. The category of emotional relatedness is often the way couples define their relationship with men in heterosexual contexts, and often it obscures all of the other categories that organize a couple's life. As therapists, we have often relied on different aspects of emotionality to shift a couple, join with them or teach emotional understanding of the other. This does a great disservice to both partners, especially the partner with less power, because it colludes with and relies solely on the feminine value of compassion and relational ability to resolve *all* aspects of the relationship. You seem to provide a context of support and caring within which you raise all of the difficult and hidden aspects of organization within a couple's life. While feminist family therapy has addressed the ethics of expanding the context of a couple's life beyond emotional intimacy, to include issues pertaining to the second shift, money, child care, and work, the fundamental structures that organize couplehood are not deconstructed with any regularity. Within the category of sexuality for example, we know that men are introduced to pornography during adolescence and earlier today, and use it to varying degrees into their adult relationships with extremely deleterious effects on their partners. Sexual practices exist from the rampant use of "on-line" pornography to corporate sex entertainment to S/M as the most extreme expression of sex domination and subordination. Millions of women lose their life savings while their male partners engage in these sexual activities. Furthermore, these women are continuously placed at risk for contracting HIV. While many feminists, particularly in the lesbian community, believe it is a personal right to freedom to choose whatever form of sexuality one desires, I believe this analysis lacks a connectedness with global politics of capitalism with respect to sex clubs, pornography, S/M clubs and sex industry workers. In particular it lacks a clear social analysis of power within the interior of a couple's relationship. The analysis rests on assumptions of consenting adults, often based on individual/interpersonal contexts of relationship. We have an ethical obligation to inquire about sexual practices beyond "frequency" and style with both heterosexual and gay couples. Nevertheless, sexuality is only one of about eight categories that organize intimate partnering as you describe in your analysis.

This piece *does* do an excellent job of contextualizing masculinity and interweaving heterosexist versus homosexual assumptions about it. It speaks more than the other pieces to some of the specific cultural differences in definitions of masculinity and particularly underlines the contradictory pressures contained in those definitions. The inclusion of the personal ads was very effective in demonstrating the intersection of "isms"–racism, sexism, ageism, heterosexism and homophobia that is internalized. You also speak more specifically to the positive characteristics of masculinity—what we might look to incorporate in evolving definitions.

In response to your opening, it is pertinent to question what would be different if women did define femininity? What would be different if they defined masculinity? Perhaps even the advances of the feminist movement have failed to offer a socially sanctioned definition of feminine character or qualities. The men's movement has really only begun to touch on newer constructions of maleness.

Your analysis of Case A explores the dimensions of power in the relationship between Lucas and Shendi and between Lucas and the culture. You use video clips to heighten Lucas' awareness of the racism affecting his life. You make the point, however, that racism, sexism and oppression at all levels are at issue in this case and seem to suggest that an exploration and expansion of Lucas' ideas about masculinity in this context *are* the treatment.

While your revised comments have explained the Cultural Context Model and the rationale behind the various types of questions you would pose to the couple, some of us remain slightly uncomfortable about some of the questions you outline, such as those about S/M and the more intimate aspects of the couple's sexual relationship. Sexuality provides a very accurate lens for understanding power dynamics in the couple, but how would you frame the necessity for posing these questions which could be quite alienating to clients? Though, again, we don't know exactly what the presenting problem was as stated by the clients, how would you justify to them your line of questioning if it doesn't fit with their definition of the problem? For instance, how do you know that Lucas *is* involved with traditionally female household tasks? For that matter, would you assume that Shendi is without first exploring their views on role performance?

You explore the gamut of masculinity with Michael and Antonio, including the dimensions of power and control. It is important to decipher the couple's ideas about who has more control within the relationship and particularly important to know what concepts of sexuality and non-exclusivity may inform their partnership, since it is in this arena that gay men differ most from heterosexual men in their values and assumptions about committed relationships. You indicate that you would explore the dimension of intimate violence, which is an important factor not to overlook in gay couples. Contextualizing the relationship in terms of larger sociopolitical issues is important, but one might still want to join with each man around his respective discomfort about the conflicts in the relationship. Any relationship, gay or straight, abusive or not, can benefit from some modeling of empathic responsiveness, since there *is* an interior dimension to the relationship and empathy is one form of intervention with power dynamics. Collaboration, negotiation and responsive empathy are important parts of a more positive construction of masculinity.

CONCLUSION

These cases and the responses to them demonstrate both the complexity of gender issues and the power of cultural norms to shape responses to the problems clients experience. Sometimes it is the cultural norms themselves that become the problem. A first step in creating change in norms regarding gender lies in an evolving consciousness of the straight-jacket that gender norms and heterosexism impose. As Stoltenberg says in *Refusing to Be a Man*:

> Male sexual identity is not a 'role.'
> Male sexual identity is not a trait.
> Male sexual identity–the belief that one is male, the belief that there is a male sex, the belief that one belongs to it–is a politically constructed idea.
> This means that masculinity is an ethical construction . . . So long as we try to act as *men* in order to try to be men. . . . we doom women to injustice . . .
> Male sexual identity is constructed through the choices we make and the actions we take.

> (Stoltenberg, 1989, p. 185)

In this sense, therapy becomes one vehicle for the reconstruction of male identity. It challenges roles, it positions itself as a commentator on the structural aspects of class and culture that intersect with gender to create oppression. Our therapy must be culturally conscious and it must promote values more in keeping with changing, positive role definitions for both men and women. These values would include mandates for collaboration, partnership, equality, and relational rather than functional competence.

In raising clients' consciousness about power inequities and the ways that they are situated in a larger community that shapes their conflicts with one another, we carry out one of the most radical functions of therapy–which is to free our clients as well as ourselves from the ongoing oppressions of culture.

Traditional Norms of Masculinity

Robert-Jay Green

The list of norms in the Appendix to this article is a distillation of ideas from many other sources in the profeminist men's studies literature (see especially Bograd, 1991; Kimmel, 1987; Kimmel & Messner, 1996; Levant & Pollack, 1995; and Pleck, 1981). Readers are encouraged to study these primary sources to expand their understanding of the material condensed here.

Different males are subject to these normative pressures in varying degrees depending on their age, race, ethnicity, geographical region, occupation, and educational level, and their family and peer group's ideas about gender relations. In addition, as Pleck (1981) has discussed, some of these norms are mutually contradictory, and attempts to conform to them are often destructive to the self or others.

In addition to its use by professionals, the list in the Appendix can be used as a handout for self-assessment and goal-setting with participants in men's groups and clients in counseling or therapy. It also can be used to help people think about the behavior and attitudes of other men and boys in their families, peer groups, or work settings.

Robert-Jay Green, PhD, is Professor and Coordinator of Family/Child Psychology Training, California School of Professional Psychology-Berkeley/Alameda.

Address correspondence to Robert-Jay Green, PhD, California School of Professional Psychology, 1005 Atlantic Avenue, Alameda, CA 94501 (E-mail: rjgreen@compuserve.com).

[Haworth co-indexing entry note]: "Traditional Norms of Masculinity." Green, Robert-Jay. Co-published simultaneously in *Journal of Feminist Family Therapy* (The Haworth Press, Inc.) Vol. 10, No. 1, 1998, pp. 81-83; and: *Transformations of Gender and Race: Family and Developmental Perspectives* (ed: Rhea V. Almeida) The Haworth Press, Inc., 1998, pp. 81-83. Single or multiple copies of this article are available for a fee from The Haworth Document Delivery Service [1-800-342-9678, 9:00 a.m. - 5:00 p.m. (EST). E-mail address: getinfo@haworthpressinc.com].

DISCUSSION

The list of norms in the Appendix is a condensation of ideas from many sources in the profeminist men's studies literature (see especially Bograd, 1991; Kimmel, 1987; Kimmel & Messner, 1996; Levant & Pollack, 1995; and Pleck, 1981).

Different males are subject to these normative pressures in varying degrees depending on their age, race, ethnicity, geographical region, occupation, education, and family and peer group's ideas and practices about gender relations. Also, some of these norms are mutually contradictory, and attempts to conform to them are often destructive to the self or others (Pleck, 1981).

In addition to its use by professionals, the list can be given to participants in men's groups and to clients in counseling or therapy for self-assessment and goal-setting. It also can be used to help people think about the way other males in their own peer groups, work settings, or families (such as their fathers or sons) are socialized to conform or allowed to diverge from the traditional normative standards.

REFERENCES

Bograd, M. (1991). *Feminist approaches for men in family therapy.* Binghamton, NY: Harrington Park Press.

Kimmel, M.S. (Ed.). (1987). *Changing men: New directions in research on men and masculinity.* Newbury Park, CA: Sage Publications.

Kimmel, M.S., & Messner, M.A. (Eds.). (1996). *Men's lives (3rd edition).* New York: Macmillan.

Levant, R.F., & Pollack, W.S. (Eds.). (1995). *A new psychology of men.* New York: Basic Books.

Pleck, J.H. (1981). *The myth of masculinity.* Cambridge, MA: MIT Press.

APPENDIX

Traditional Norms of Masculinity

1. *Suppression of emotional vulnerability*; emotional distance; avoidance of painful feelings in self and others (fear, grief, hurt, sadness); emphasis on logic, rationality, and emotional restraint.
2. *Avoiding feminine behavior* and activities traditionally associated with women's role (such as housework, childcare, gender nonconforming leisure activities and occupations).
3. *Primacy of work role*; seeking power, admiration, and social status through achievement; self-esteem primarily based on work performance; willingness to sacrifice personal well-being and relationships in order to succeed at work and earn money.
4. *Independence*; avoidance and denial of dependency on others; withdrawal and isolation rather than seeking help, nurturance, or guidance from others.
5. *Aggression* used as a means to control others and as a means of conflict resolution.
6. *Toughness*, stoicism, projecting an air of confidence in the face of adversity, danger, or physical pain.
7. *Striving for dominance* and hierarchical authority in relationships; patriarchal control and leadership in family.
8. *Provider/protector* for others in family.
9. *Treating sexual partners as objects*; emphasis on rigid normative standards of beauty; using partner as a "trophy"; nonmutual approaches to sexuality; emphasis on sexual prowess and performance.
10. *Homophobia* (irrational fear/anger at gay men and lesbians; avoidance of emotional closeness and affection with other males).

Finding the Words:
Instruments
for a Therapy of Liberation

Roberto Font
Ken Dolan-Del Vecchio
Rhea V. Almeida

Most psychotherapeutic approaches involve conversations in which societally mandated hierarchies of power are rarely mentioned and even more rarely challenged. For example, a heterosexual couple seeking assistance for a "communication problem" is typically engaged in an exploration that, in keeping with their expectations, locates their problem within the bounds of their "personality-based" dyadic system. The therapist proceeds as though only the emotional dimension of the couple's partnership is significant. Consequently, questions about the management of money; second shift responsibilities such as housework, childcare, and maintenance of the couple's connections to family and friends; decision making and conflict resolution patterns; and how the couple negotiates fulfillment of each partner's sexual needs are not routinely asked. If one or both members of the couple are people of color it is likely that the impact of racism both outside and within the couple system will go unexplored.

Roberto Font, LCSW, is Co-Director, Institute for Family Services, Somerset, NJ. Ken Dolan-Del Vecchio, LCSW, is a Faculty Member, Institute for Family Services, Somerset, NJ. Rhea V. Almeida, PhD, is Founder and Executive Director, Institute for Family Services, 3 Clyde Road, Suite 101, Somerset, NJ 08873, and Faculty Member, Family Institute of New Jersey, Metuchen, NJ.

[Haworth co-indexing entry note]: "Finding the Words: Instruments for a Therapy of Liberation." Font, Roberto, Ken Dolan-Del Vecchio, and Rhea V. Almeida. Co-published simultaneously in *Journal of Feminist Family Therapy* (The Haworth Press, Inc.) Vol. 10, No. 1, 1998, pp. 85-97; and: *Transformations of Gender and Race: Family and Developmental Perspectives* (ed: Rhea V. Almeida) The Haworth Press, Inc., 1998, pp. 85-97. Single or multiple copies of this article are available for a fee from The Haworth Document Delivery Service [1-800-342-9678, 9:00 a.m. - 5:00 p.m. (EST). E-mail address: getinfo@haworthpressinc.com].

Similarly, if the couple is homosexual it is likely that the impact of homophobia will go largely unexplored. The focus will be kept upon the verbal/emotional transactions that the couple describes and exhibits during the therapy session.

It is also likely that the therapist will actively enforce societal prescriptions in a multitude of ways within the therapeutic contact. For example, it is likely that the therapist will be looking for psychopathology in one or both members of the couple. Since most diagnoses were developed by men and "for" women, it is likely that a female client will be more perniciously diagnosed. Similarly, it is likely, in keeping with societally prescribed expectations, that the woman's emotionality and not the man's lack of emotionality will be labeled problematic (Kupers, 1993, 1995). The list of ways that therapists replicate and reinforce societally prescribed social norms within the therapy session, often to the serious detriment of their clients, is nearly infinite (Almeida, 1993; Chesler, 1989). The most dangerous examples, of course, include those in which therapists hold women clients responsible for their own physical battering by abusive partners (Stark and Flitcraft, 1995; Dolan-Del Vecchio, 1998).

A central aspect of the Cultural Context Model (Almeida, Font, Messineo, Woods, 1998) is socioeducation, within which elemental aspects of the hierarchies of power and privilege governing social interaction at all systems levels are examined. Because hierarchies of power are organized around maintaining the privilege of dominant collectives and because language develops within and is a primary tool for maintaining social structures, there is a dearth of language for describing the experiences of less dominant groups and for describing the elemental structures and patterned processes of domination from the perspectives of those who are oppressed. Simply stated, it is in the interest of dominant groups for their experiences of privilege and the experiences of those who are oppressed by these privileges to remain linguistically invisible. That which is "unspeakable" cannot be challenged. A second line of linguistic defense for dominant norms is the myth teaching us to believe that those patterns which are pervasive and ubiquitous are "natural," i.e., men are "naturally" aggressive, and it is therefore unnecessary to develop a language for inquiry regarding these norms. The development of complex language centered upon these aspects of life creates the potential to raise questions regarding the true nature of such patterns and the range of options in existence.

Initially, therefore, socioeducation requires the provision of a conceptual frame and language for understanding and describing daily experiences that derive from our social locations within hierarchies of power and privilege.

> Power differences between men and women as groups are not always experienced at the individual level. This is due to the kinds of social relations that exist between men and women. Unlike other dominant and subordinate groups, strong emotional attachment, mutual caring, and shared dependence link individual men and women–so complicating experiences of power and domination for both. (Bograd, 1991)

Power and control wheels (see Cultural Context Model, 1992, Figures 1-4) help to clarify these experiences by systematically delineating at both the private/couple systems level and the public/communal systems level the ways that differences of gender, race, and sexual orientation contribute to predictable and patterned differences in access to power and privileges, including safety. The "Private Domain of Abuse Within Heterosexual Relationships," (Figure 1) for example, tracks into the interior of private relationships the impacts of the power differences and role prescriptions for men and women operating within the public world. It describes 10 categories that fundamentally organize the power dynamics within intimate partnering. Similarly, the "Expanded Male Norms" (see Appendix) adapted from the "Ten Traditional Norms of Masculinity" (Green, 1998), moves beyond traditional role prescriptions for men by describing accountability-based and nurturant relational patterns for men to work toward.

Any discussion about the private experiences within a particular family or about a man's definition of masculinity and his experiences in attempting to fulfill this definition needs to be contextualized. For example, the dominant prescriptions for masculinity are essentially white, middle-class, heterosexual standards. Men of color are assaulted on a daily basis within the public world and these assaults include institutional barriers to fulfilling their role as breadwinner. These realities need to be acknowledged as one explores the ways that such men attempt to fulfill their prescribed masculine roles. For example, in response to racist assaults within their daily public experiences, some men of color rigidify their authoritarianism and control within the realm of couple and family relationships.

Similarly, the interior lives of gay and lesbian couples and their families need to be contextualized by an exploration of the virulence of life within a society pervaded by homophobia (Figure 2). The interior lives of white families need to be explored within a conversation that identifies the ways that privilege and acknowledgment within the public world contribute to

FIGURE 1. Private Context: The Misuse and Abuse of Power Within Heterosexual Relationships

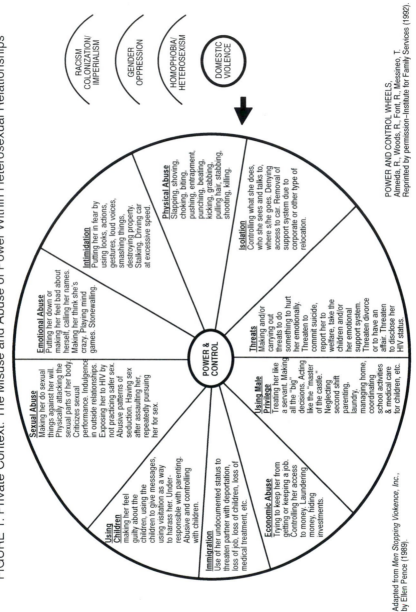

RACISM COLONIZATION/ IMPERIALISM

GENDER OPPRESSION

HOMOPHOBIA/ HETEROSEXISM

DOMESTIC VIOLENCE

POWER & CONTROL

Emotional Abuse
Putting her down or making her feel bad about herself, calling her names. Making her think she's crazy. Playing mind games. Stonewalling.

Intimidation
Putting her in fear by using looks, actions, gestures, loud voices, smashing things, destroying property. Stalking. Driving car at excessive speed.

Physical Abuse
Slapping, shoving, choking, biting, pushing, entrapment, punching, beating, kicking, grabbing, pulling hair, stabbing, shooting, killing.

Isolation
Controlling what she does, who she sees and talks to, where s/he goes. Denying access to car. Removal of support system due to corporate or other type of relocation.

Sexual Abuse
Making her do sexual things against her will. Physically attacking the sexual parts of her body. Criticizes sexual performance. Indulgence in outside relationships. Exposing her to HIV by not practicing safer sex. Abusive patterns of seduction. Having sex after assaulting her, repeatedly pursuing her for sex.

Threats
Making and/or carrying out threats to do something to hurt her emotionally. Threaten to commit suicide, report her to welfare, take the children and/or her emotional support system. Threaten divorce or to have an affair. Threaten to disclose her HIV status.

Using Children
making her feel guilty about the children, using the children to give messages, using visitation as a way to harass her. Under-responsible with parenting. Abusive and controlling with children.

Using Male Privilege
Treating her like a servant. Making all the "big" decisions. Acting like the "master of the castle." Neglecting second shift parenting, laundry, managing home, coordinating school activities & medical care for children, etc.

Immigration
Use of her undocumented status to threaten partner with deportation, loss of job, loss of children, loss of medical treatment, etc.

Economic Abuse
Trying to keep her from getting or keeping a job. Controlling her access to money. Laundering money, hiding investments.

POWER AND CONTROL WHEELS,
Almeida, R., Woods, R., Font, R., Messineo, T.
Reprinted by permission–Institute for Family Services (1992).

Adapted from *Men Stopping Violence, Inc.,*
by Ellen Pence (1989).

FIGURE 2. Private Context: The Misuse and Abuse of Power Within Lesbian and Gay Relationships

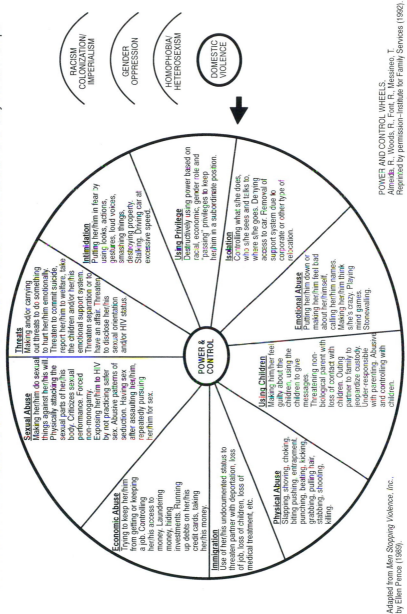

RACISM
COLONIZATION/
IMPERIALISM

GENDER
OPPRESSION

HOMOPHOBIA/
HETEROSEXISM

DOMESTIC
VIOLENCE

**POWER &
CONTROL**

Threats
Making and/or carrying out threats to do something to hurt her/him emotionally. Threaten to commit suicide. Threaten to report her/him to welfare, take the children and/or her/his emotional support system. Threaten separation or to have an affair. Threaten to disclose her/his sexual orientation and/or HIV status.

Intimidation
Putting her/him in fear by using looks, actions, gestures, loud voices, smashing things, destroying property. Stalking. Driving car at excessive speed.

Using Privilege
Destructively using power based on racial, economic, gender role and "passing" privileges to keep her/him in a subordinate position.

Isolation
Controlling what s/he does, who s/he sees and talks to, where s/he goes. Denying access to car. Removal of support system due to corporate or other type of relocation.

Emotional Abuse
Putting her/him down or making her/him feel bad about her/himself, calling her/him names. Making her/him think s/he's crazy. Playing mind games. Stonewalling.

Sexual Abuse
Making her/him do sexual things against her/his will. Physically attacking the sexual parts of her/his body. Criticizes sexual performance. Forced non-monogamy. Exposing her/him to HIV by not practicing safer sex. Abusive patterns of seduction. Having sex after assaulting her/him, repeatedly pursuing her/him for sex.

Using Children
Making him/her feel guilty about the children, using the children to give messages. Threatening non-biological parent with loss of contact with children. Outing partner to family to jeopardize custody. Under-responsible and controlling with parenting. Abusive and controlling with children.

Economic Abuse
Trying to keep her/him from getting or keeping a job. Controlling her/his access to money. Laundering money, hiding investments. Running up debts on her/his credit cards, taking her/his money.

Immigration
Use of her/his undocumented status to threaten partner with deportation, loss of job, loss of children, loss of medical treatment, etc.

Physical Abuse
Slapping, shoving, choking, biting pushing, entrapment, punching, beating, kicking, grabbing, pulling hair, stabbing, shooting, killing.

Adapted from *Men Stopping Violence, Inc.*, by Ellen Pence (1989).

POWER AND CONTROL WHEELS.
Almeida, R., Woods, R., Font, R., Messineo, T.
Reprinted by permission–Institute for Family Services (1992).

FIGURE 3. Public Context: The Misuse and Abuse of Power Towards People of Color

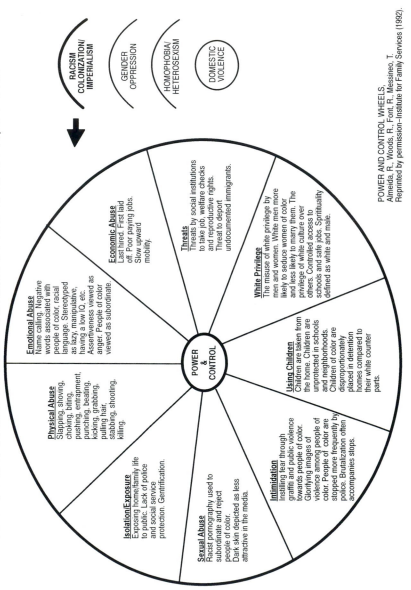

RACISM COLONIZATION/ IMPERIALISM

GENDER OPPRESSION

HOMOPHOBIA/ HETEROSEXISM

DOMESTIC VIOLENCE

POWER & CONTROL

Emotional Abuse
Name calling. Negative words associated with people of color, racial language. Stereotyped as lazy, manipulative, having a low IQ, etc. Assertiveness viewed as anger. People of color viewed as subordinate.

Economic Abuse
Last hired. First laid off. Poor paying jobs. Slow upward mobility.

Threats
Threats by social institutions to take job, welfare checks and reproductive rights. Threat to deport undocumented immigrants.

White Privilege
The misuse of white privilege by men and women. White men more likely to seduce women of color and less likely to marry them. The privilege of white culture over others. Controlled access to schools and safe jobs. Spirituality defined as white and male.

Using Children
Children are taken from the home. Children are unprotected in schools and neighborhoods. Children of color are disproportionately placed in detention homes compared to their white counter parts.

Physical Abuse
Slapping, shoving, choking, biting, pushing, entrapment, punching, beating, kicking, grabbing, pulling hair, stabbing, shooting, killing.

Isolation/Exposure
Exposing home/family life to public. Lack of police and social service protection. Gentrification.

Sexual Abuse
Racist pornography used to subordinate and reject people of color. Dark skin depicted as less attractive in the media.

Intimidation
Instilling fear through graffiti and public violence towards people of color. Glorifying images of violence among people of color. People of color are stopped more frequently by police. Brutalization often accompanies stops.

POWER AND CONTROL WHEELS,
Almeida, R., Woods, R., Font, R, Messineo, T.
Reprinted by permission–Institute for Family Services (1992).

FIGURE 4. Private Context: The Misuse and Abuse of Power Towards Lesbians and Gays

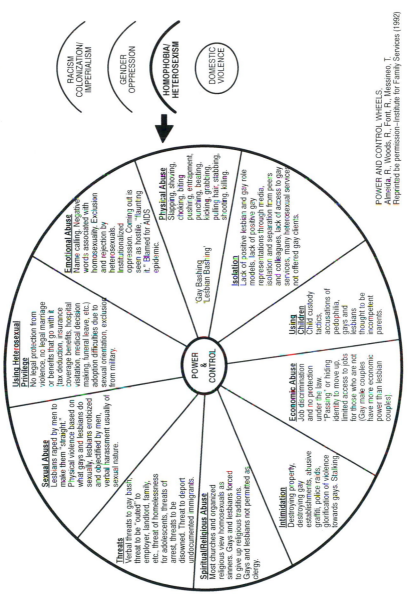

RACISM COLONIZATION/ IMPERIALISM

GENDER OPPRESSION

HOMOPHOBIA/ HETEROSEXISM

DOMESTIC VIOLENCE

Using Heterosexual Privilege
No legal protection from violence, no legal marriage or benefits that go with it (tax deduction, insurance coverage benefits, hospital visitation, medical decision making, funeral leave, etc.) adoption difficulties due to sexual orientation, exclusion from military.

Emotional Abuse Name calling. Negative words associated with homosexuality. Exclusion and rejection by heterosexuals. Institutionalized oppression. Coming out is seen as hostile. "Flaunting it." Blamed for AIDS epidemic.

Physical Abuse Slapping, shoving, choking, biting pushing, entrapment, punching, beating, kicking, grabbing, pulling hair, stabbing, shooting, killing.

'Gay Bashing' 'Lesbian Bashing'

Isolation Lack of positive lesbian and gay role models, lack of positive gay representations through media, isolation and separation from peers and colleagues, lack of access to gay services, many heterosexual services not offered gay clients.

POWER & CONTROL

Sexual Abuse Lesbians raped by men to make them "straight." Physical violence based on what gays and lesbians do sexually, lesbians eroticized and objectified by men, verbal harassment usually of sexual nature.

Using Children Child custody tactics, accusations of pedophilia, gays and lesbians thought to be incompetent parents.

Threats Verbal threats to gay bash, threat to be "outed" to employer, landlord, family, etc., threat of homelessness for adolescents, threats of arrest, threats to be disowned. Threat to deport undocumented immigrants.

Economic Abuse Job discrimination and no protection under the law. "Passing" or hiding identity to move up, limited access to jobs for those who are not (Gay male couples have more economic power than lesbian couples).

Spiritual/Religious Abuse Most churches and organized religious view homosexuals as sinners. Gays and lesbians forced to give up religious traditions. Gays and lesbians not permitted as clergy.

Intimidation Destroying property, destroying gay establishments, abusive graffiti, police raids, glorification of violence towards gays. Stalking.

POWER AND CONTROL WHEELS,
Almeida, R., Woods, R., Font, R., Messineo, T.
Reprinted be permission–Institute for Family Services (1992)

91

the expectations and range of options available within the private realm of family life. In addition to race and sexual orientation, other differences, such as class, ethnicity, age, and ability, contribute additional layers of complexity to the conversation. The following are essential readings on the complex linkages of diversity and adversity at the interface of the public and private contexts: Almeida, Woods, Messineo, Font, and Heer (1994), Becker (1997), Berube (1997), Chin (1997), Cose (1993), Crenshaw (1991, 1993, 1994), Dyson (1996), Gates (1997), Gates and West (1996), Haley and X (1964), McCall (1995), Mann (1997), Vazquez (1997), and Walker (1997).

The "Public Domain" (Figures 3 and 4) wheels provide a framework and language for describing institutional violence perpetrated within the public world against marginalized groups. As such, they provide a starting point for the conversations described above–essential therapeutic conversations which connect the private experiences of families to their larger societal context.

While they are not presented within the collection that follows, we have also developed culture specific female norms.

These power and control wheels as well as the list of expanded male norms are used with individuals, couples, families and groups. It is helpful for men and women in families as well as within other contexts, such as at work, to dismantle the multiple ways in which their lives are organized. Referring to these sheets, participants are able to look beyond the traditional therapeutic focus, which attempts to locate issues and conflicts primarily within individual (generally female) personalities and dyadic exchanges. As the frame is enlarged such that it begins to survey the role prescriptions and power dynamics connected to differences such as gender, race, sexual orientation and class, an entirely different kind of therapeutic conversation emerges. Within this new conversation the focus moves away from the search for pathology and toward the search for justice.

REFERENCES AND SUGGESTED READINGS
ON MASCULINITIES

Almeida, R., Woods, R., Messineo, T., Font, R. (1998). *The Cultural Context Model: An overview.* In McGoldrick, M. (Ed.). Revisioning Family Therapy: Race, Culture and Gender in Clinical Practice. New York: Guilford.

Almeida, R. (1996). *Asian Indian Families: Hindu/Christian/Muslim.* In McGoldrick, M., Giordano, J., and Pierce, J.K. (Eds.). Ethnicity & Family Therapy, Second Edition. New York: Guilford Press.

Almeida, R., Wood, R., Messineo, T., Font, R. & Heer, C. (1994). *Violence in the Lives of the Racially and Sexually Different: A public and private dilemma. Journal of Feminist Family Therapist,* Vol. 5(3/4).

Almeida, R. (1993). Unexamined assumptions and service delivery systems: Feminist theory and racial exclusions. *Journal of Feminist Family Therapy.* Vol. 5(1), 3-23.

Becker, D.P. (1997). *Growing Up in Two Closets: Class and Privilege in the Lesbian and Gay Community.* In Raffo, S. (Ed.). Queerly Classed: Gay Men and Lesbians Write About Class. Boston: South End Press.

Berube, A. (1997). *Intellectual Desire.* In Raffo, S. (Ed.). Queerly Classed: Gay and Lesbians Write About Class. Boston: South End Press.

Bograd, M. (1991). *Feminist Approaches for Men in Family Therapy.* New York: Harrington Park Press.

Boyd-Franklin, N. (1989). *Black Families in Therapy.* New York: Guilford.

Buchwald, F., Fletcher, P.R. & Roth, M. (1993). *Transforming a Rape Culture.* Minnesota: Milkweed Editions.

Cashorali, P. (1995). *Fairy Tales: Traditional Stories Retold for Gay Men.* New York: HarperCollins.

Chesler, P. (1989). *Women and Madness.* San Diego: Harcourt Brace.

Chin, J. (1997). *Currency.* In Raffo, S. (Ed.). Queerly Classed: Gay Men and Lesbians Write About Class. Boston: South End Press.

Churchill, W. (1996). *Indian "R" Us? Reflections on the "Men's Movement."* In From a Native Son: Selected Essays on Indigenism.

Cose, F. (1993). *The Rage of a Privileged Class: Why Are Middle-Class Blacks Angry? Why Should America Care?* New York: HarperCollins.

Crenshaw, K. (1993). Race, Gender, and Violence Against Women: Convergences, Divergences and Other Black Feminist Conundrums. In Marion, M. (Ed.), *Family Matters: Readings on Family Lives and the Law.* New York: The New Press.

Crenshaw, K.W. (1994). Mapping the Margins: Intersectionality, Identity Politics, and Violence Against Women of Color. In Fineman, M.A. & Mykitiuk, R. (Eds.), *The Public Nature of Private Violence.* New York: Routledge.

Crenshaw, K. (1991). *Speech at the Forum for Women State Legislators. 11/15/91.* San Diego.

Denborough, D. (1994). *A model of hope: Men against sexual assault–Accountability Structures.* In Dulwich Centre Newsletter No. 2&3, pp. 44-54.

Dolan-Del Vecchio, K. (1996). The Foundation for Accountability: A Linking of Many Different Voices. *American Family Therapy Academy (AFTA) Newsletter.* No. 64, pp. 20-23.

Dolan-Del Vecchio, K. (1998). Dismantling White Male Privilege Within Family Therapy. In McGoldrick, M. (Ed.). *Revisioning Family Therapy: Race, Culture, and Gender in Clinical Practice.* New York: Guilford Press.

Dworkin, A. (1997). *Life and Death: Unapologetic Writings on the Continuing War Against Women.* New York: The Free Press.

Dyson, M.E. (1996). *Between God & Gangsta.* New York: Oxford Press.

Edwards, T. (1994). *Erotics & Politics: Gay male sexuality, masculinity and feminism.* New York: Routledge.

Elliott, P. (1996). *Shattering Illusions: Same-Sex Domestic Violence.* In Renzetti, C.M. & Miley, C.H. (Eds.). Violence in Gay and Lesbian Domestic Partnerships. New York: Harrington Park Press.

Ferber, A.L. (1995). *Shame of White Men: Interracial Sexuality and the Construction of White Masculinity in Contemporary White Supremacist Discourse.* Masculinities, Vol. 3(2), pp. 1-24.

Fuentes, C. (1988). *How I started to write.* In R. Simonson & S. Walker (Eds.), The graywolf annual five: multicultural literacy. Minnesota: Graywolf Press.

Gates, H.L. and West, C. (1996). *The Future of the Race.* New York: Vintage.

Gates, H. (1997). *Thirteen Ways of looking at a black man.* New York: Random House.

Green, R.-J. (1997). *Ten Traditional Norms of Masculinity.* (Printed in this volume.)

Grossman, D. (1995). *On Killing: The Psychological Cost of Learning to Kill in War and Society.* New York: Little Brown and Company.

Haley, A. and X, M. (1964). *The Autobiography of Malcolm X.* New York: Ballantine Books.

hooks, b. and West, C. (1991). *Breaking Bread: Insurgent Black Intellectual Life.* Boston: South End Press.

Kimmel, M. (1995). *The Politics of Manhood.* Philadelphia: Temple University Press.

Kimmel, M. (1996). *Manhood in America: A Cultural History.* New York: Free Press.

Kivel, P. (1992). *Men's Work: How to Stop the Violence That Tears Our Lives Apart.* Minnesota: Hazeldon.

Kohlberg, L. (1969). *Stage and Sequence: The cognitive developmental approach to socialization.* In D. Goslin (Ed.), The handbook of socialization theory and research. Chicago, Illinois: Rand McNally.

Kohlberg, L. (1981). *The philosophy of moral development: Moral stages and the idea of justice*: Essays on moral development, I. California: Harper & Row.

Kupers, T.A. (1995). *The Politics of Psychiatry: Gender and Sexual Preference in DSM-IV.* Masculinities, Vol. 3(2), pp. 67-78.

Kupers, T. (1993). *Revisioning Men's Lives: Gender, Intimacy, and Power.* New York: Guilford.

Laird, J. and Green, R.-J. (1996). *Lesbians and Gays in Couples and Families: A Handbook for Therapists.* San Francisco: Jossey-Bass.

Maccoby, E.E. (1990). *Gender and relationships: A developmental account.* American Psychologist, Vol. 45, pp. 513-520.

Maduro, O. (1995). *Directions for a Reassessment of Latina/o Religion.* In Stevens-Arroyo, A.M. & Perez Y Mena, A.T. (Eds.), Syncretism with African and Indigenous Peoples' Religions Among Latinos. New York: The Bildner Center for Western Hemisphere Studies.

Majors, R., & Billison, J.M., (1992). *Cool Pose.* New York: Macmillan Inc.

Mann, W.J. (1997). A Boy's Own Class. In Raffo, S. (Ed.), *Queerly Classed: Gay Men and Lesbians Write About Class*. Boston: South End Press. 217-226.

McCall, N. (1995). *Makes Me Wanna Holler: A Young Black Man in America*. New York: Vintage Books.

Miedzian, M. (1991). *Boys will be Boys–Breaking the Link between Masculinity and Violence*. New York: Doubleday.

Pasick, R. (1992). *Awakening from the Deep Sleep: A Powerful Guide for Courageous Men*. San Francisco: HarperCollins.

Ratti, L. (1993). Feminism & Men. In *A Lotus of Another Color–An Unfolding of South Asian Gays & Lesbian Experience*. Boston MA: Alyson Publications.

Rofes, E. (1997). *Academics as Bears: Thoughts on Middleclass Erotization of Working Men's Bodies*. In L. Wright (Eds.), The Bear Book. New York: Harrington Park Press.

Sadownick, D. (1996). *Sex Between Men*. New York: HarperCollins Publisher.

Siegel, S. and Lowe, E. (1995). *Uncharted Lives: Understanding the Life Passages of Gay Men*. New York: Plume/Penguin.

Vazquez, C. (1997). Spirit and Passion. In Raffo, S. (Ed.), *Queerly Classed: Gay Men and Lesbians Write About Class*. Boston: South End Press. 121-134.

Stark, E. & Flitcraft, A. (1995). Personal Power and Institutional Victimization: Treating the Dual Trauma of Woman Battering. *Post Traumatic Therapy and Victims of Violence*. 115-151.

Stoltenberg, J. (1989). *Refusing to be a man: essays on sex and justice*. New York: Meridian.

Straton, J. (1994). *Research note: The myth of the "battered husband syndrome."* Masculinities. Vol. 2, No. 4, pp. 79-82.

Tomasese, K. & Waldegrave, C. (1993). *Cultural and Gender Accountability in the "Just Therapy" Approach. Journal of Feminist Family Therapy*. Vol. 5(2), pp. 29-45.

Vazquez, C. (1997). Spirit and Passion. In Raffo, S. (Ed.), *Queerly Classed: Gay Men and Lesbians Write About Class*. Boston: South End Press. 121-134.

Walker, A. (1983). *The Divided Life of Jean Toomer*. In: In Search of Our Mother's Gardens: Womanist Prose. San Diego: Harcourt Brace.

Walker, A. (1983). *Lulls*. In Search of Our Mother's Gardens: Womanist Prose. San Diego: Harcourt Brace.

Walker, A. (1983). *Brothers and Sisters*. In Search of Our Mother's Gardens: Womanist Prose. San Diego: Harcourt Brace.

Walker, A. (1983). *The Same River Twice: Honoring the Difficult*. New York: Washington Square Press.

Walker, A. (1997). *What That Day Was Like for Me: The Million Man March, October 16, 1995: The Flowering of Black Men*. In Anything We Love Can Be Saved: A Writer's Activism. New York: Random House.

Walker, A. (1997). *This Side of Glory: The Autobiography of David Hilliard and the Story of the Black Panther Party by David Hilliard & Lewis Cole*. In

Anything We Love Can Be Saved: A Writer's Activism. New York: Random House.

Walker, A. (1997). *Letter to the International Indian Treaty Council.* In Anything We Love Can Be Saved: A Writer's Activism. New York: Random House.

West, C. (1993). *Race Matters.* New York: Vintage Books.

APPENDIX

EXPANDED NORMS OF THE MALE ROLE

Font, Dolan-Del Vecchio, and Almeida

1. *Expanded emotionality:* the willingness to express the full range of emotions, including exuberance, joy, love, wonder and awe at things beautiful, fear, sadness, remorse, disappointment, and all the rest.
2. *Embracing femininity:* valuing qualities and activities traditionally considered feminine (household and childcare tasks; cooking, creating art, dancing, and composing poetry; human service occupations).
3. *Balancing work and family life:* Seeking pride through contributing both within the world of work and as an active participant in family life.
4. *Embracing relatedness over individualism:* valuing interdependence with all other human beings and with the rest of the natural world.
5. *Valuing collaboration:* using consensus building as a primary means for conflict resolution.
6. *Maintaining flexibility:* when faced with adversity, demonstrating respect for the opinions of others alongside assertiveness regarding one's own ideas, emotional availability, and emotional vulnerability.
7. *Valuing shared power of relatedness:* striving to create equal partnerships with adults and relationships with children that engender feelings of being loved and respected while also providing appropriate limits and structure.
8. *Relational attitude toward sexuality:* participation that affords each partner safety, dignity, and pleasure. Respect for others.
9. *Overcoming heterosexism/homophobia:* valuing difference by creating nurturing relationships with gay men, lesbians, bisexuals, and

heterosexuals and by borrowing expanded forms of participation in the following dimensions of relationships: non-threatening behavior; mutual respect; trust and support; honesty and accountability; responsible parenting; household responsibilities; economic partnership; negotiation and fairness in resolving conflicts.

Adapted from *Traditional Norms of the Male Role* (Green, 1998)

Dialogue:
Transformations of Race and Gender

Elaine Pinderhughes
Evan Imber-Black
Lynn Parker

The authors were asked by Rhea Almeida, Ph.D., to participate in a dialogue regarding transformations (or lack thereof) each have witnessed regarding race and gender. We deliberated about how to best structure the conversation. At first we thought e-mail would be more expedient. However, we finally opted for a bit more intimacy–a telephone conversation. This was later transcribed then edited by the authors. Lynn agreed to facilitate the mechanics of the conversation. She generated some initial questions. These were sent to Evan and Elaine for consideration prior to the dialogue. The dialogue commenced on November 10, 1997.

Lynn: As an overview, we have four general areas of possible discussion:

1. Where do we situate ourselves now in terms of the feminist discourse?
2. What has been the impact of feminist thought on women's lives, on practice, and in academia?
3. What is still missing? and

Elaine Pinderhughes, PhD, is affiliated with Boston University School of Social Work. Evan Imber-Black, PhD, is affiliated with the Urban Institute, Bronx, NY. Lynn Parker, PhD, is affiliated with the University of Denver, School of Social Work, Denver, CO.

[Haworth co-indexing entry note]: "Dialogue: Transformations of Race and Gender." Pinderhughes, Elaine, Evan Imber-Black, and Lynn Parker. Co-published simultaneously in *Journal of Feminist Family Therapy* (The Haworth Press, Inc.) Vol. 10, No. 1, 1998, pp. 99-111; and: *Transformations of Gender and Race: Family and Developmental Perspectives* (ed: Rhea V. Almeida) The Haworth Press, Inc., 1998, pp. 99-111. Single or multiple copies of this article are available for a fee from The Haworth Document Delivery Service [1-800-342-9678, 9:00 a.m. - 5:00 p.m. (EST). E-mail address: getinfo@haworthpressinc.com].

4. What are the current power politics in the family therapy field?

In responding to the first question, I wonder if it might be helpful if each of you would begin by saying something about yourself, and any hopes or interests that led you to participate in the dialogue. Who would like to begin?

Elaine: I have never been intimately involved with the feminist movement per se. People have begun to ask me to address that, but this is new for me. I've been reading about it, and I've understood the dynamics. To a certain degree, I've always believed in those dynamics, but I do not see myself as an expert in that. I assume that I was asked to address that interface, or the overlap, or whatever you want to call it.

Lynn: Between race and gender?

Elaine: Right. I just want to say where I'm coming from.

Evan: And, I would say that in terms of where I see myself now, I certainly identify myself as part of the feminist critique in family therapy. I think my interests and my commitments include that, but are larger than that.

Elaine: Exactly.

Lynn: Could you say more about that?

Evan: In terms of race, class, gender, emphasizing, with any couple or family that I'm working with, issues of difference, both within the family and then between the family and the outside world.

Elaine: See, I've always approached this from the focus of power and lack of power from the very beginning. My initial reason for it was race. However, it soon became clear that all of the other ways that people are connected in terms of group and individual identity, as well as interaction and the roles they are put in by society–that all of these were governed by the politics of power in similar ways. And so, I was always thinking about those multiple ways that people are influenced in their various identities and connections.

Lynn: Did you see feminist thought as excluding other areas of difference in power initially?

Elaine: That was always apparent to me, you see, because I had started from the point of view of race, and I rarely saw race [being addressed]. I didn't feel it was substantially addressed until recently where people have been talking lots more about that.

Evan: Elaine, let me ask a question about that: Within family therapy, or within feminism, or both?

Elaine: I think I'm talking about feminism in general.

Evan: Okay. Because I think within family therapy, in terms of the thought that is going on in say, the last 15 years, that there was a beginning movement around feminism and around the differences in power between men and women, both in the outside world and in the family. Men and women were taken as sort of generic terms without any distinctions being drawn initially about race, about how that would change the power in couples or in the outside world, about class and so forth. Gradually, over time–and your work Elaine, has really influenced this a lot–there has been a broadening of that lens to look beyond gender and to look more at issues of race and class.

Elaine: I think we agree. You're seeing it as having happened earlier then I sensed it.

Evan: Yes.

Lynn: Evan, are you saying you see progress more in the family therapy field than more broadly?

Evan: I don't know about more broadly, I guess, because the world I travel in is the family therapy world. I must say that I'm not somebody that has kept up with all of the literature say within gender studies or feminist thought or so on,–somewhat so–but, I certainly don't consider myself an expert in that. But within the family therapy field, for instance, particularly within AFTA (American Family Therapy Academy) . . .

Elaine: Oh, absolutely with AFTA, yes.

Evan: The shifts and the struggles to begin to take seriously issues of difference and differences in power.

Elaine: I think that it is happening among women, but I wonder about the men (I am thinking especially of those who have left). I don't know whether they left because of that.

Lynn: Are you saying, left AFTA?

Elaine: Right. Am I saying something out of school now? (Laughter from all.)

Lynn: I'm interested! I've just heard of AFTA, if you can imagine.

Elaine: In terms of men (or anyone) and power, I believe that when people have power, it's really very hard for them to think about power differential and shifts. Even just giving up a little bit of power feels very depriving. It's a strange thing, and to an outsider who has little or none, it would seem as though equalizing power would be quite easy to do, but it is, in fact, a great deprivation. I've seen that in terms of others, not just men, so I'm not surprised. I guess what I'm saying is that I'm not sure that in family therapy such a shift is as fully accepted, especially among large numbers of men.

Lynn: Are you saying that what hasn't been as fully accepted is both the feminist critique and any attention to race and other power differences?

Elaine: I was just talking about feminism itself, not even to mention race. It feels to me again that men feel very attacked, doubly attacked, both in terms of being white and male. That's my perception, and I'm not talking about the people that I see in AFTA currently, but I'm talking about on a broader scale.

Lynn: Some of the dropouts, and broader than AFTA?

Evan: Yes, I would agree.

Elaine: I don't think that, in response to the feminist critique, it is any different from the white backlash. I think that the dynamics are similar. For many men, it's like power that is being eroded on two levels.

Lynn: When you say two levels, what do you mean?

Elaine: In terms of the male role and in terms of race for white men.

Lynn: If you look at how feminism was, say 15 years ago, and also race, gender, and other issues of oppression, do you see a difference between how it is now and how it was then?

Evan: In the family therapy field, or in society at large?

Lynn: Well, why don't we start with the family therapy field and then move into the broader spectrum.

Evan: I do see a difference. How deep the difference goes is hard to say. But certainly, if you look in the journals, what is being written about, the assumption of positions of influence in organizations and also on journal boards and that sort of thing, I think we would have to say that there has been a substantial shift, particularly in terms of women. When a lot of this started, I can remember some of us sitting around and trying to figure out what was the percentage of women on the various journal boards. It was very small—and on the boards of major organizations. Certainly, I think there has been a concerted effort–political organizing–to change that. So, in that sense, yes, I think there has been a change. What has been the change in the practice of family therapy? I think it's much harder to judge that because, of course, who knows what people do behind closed doors. But I think that the sensibilities of feminist thought have definitely come into the field in journal articles, books, positions of influence and so forth.

Elaine: I certainly think that is true without a doubt. In terms of AFTA, there was an enormous change.

Lynn: What changes did you see? How was it before, and how is it now?

Elaine: [Before] The leadership was almost, not totally, but predominantly male. And, [now] the new conceptualizations were formulated by women, and they are now in the organization in even larger numbers than men.

Lynn: How about women of color?

Elaine: Well, that's a little different. In AFTA, there is definitely an increase. I think AFTA has probably done better than most any other organization, except for maybe ORTHO.

Evan: I think that's true. We have a long way to go in terms of race, but I think that it's true that the commitment has been made and there are a number of people who are moving that forward. I can certainly remember (this will give you an idea, Lynn, of sort of where we've come from), in 1989 I was the program chair for AFTA's annual meeting. And, I must say without even realizing it, I chose, I think it was, 13 women and 2 men to be in prominent positions in the meeting. I was excoriated in print by Frank Pittman. And so, I went back and counted who the speakers had been in all the previous years of meetings, (which at that point was 12 or 13 years of meetings), and, of course, it was something like 80 percent men and 20 percent women. So, I called it a mid-course correction, but the flack that I took for that was enormous. Now, what it led to, in terms of it being a mid-course correction, was then a lot of attention was given to balance the program so there were sufficient numbers of women and sufficient numbers of men. Subsequently, a similar kind of effort was made around people of color; again, in sort of visible positions of being able to present their work in large plenaries, keynote addresses and so forth.

Elaine: Evan knows how to do that. She did the same thing when she was president of AFTA. She actually structured in this change, which was an absolutely magnificent move that she made.

Evan: Well, thanks, Elaine. A lot of that was in motion before I ever became president of AFTA. The organization had made those kinds of commitments when Rachel Hare-Mustin, Froma Walsh, and Dick Chase were presidents, and now it has been a question of carrying that forth. But again, the question that it raises for me is what is happening in practice, and I wish I knew more what people are actually doing in the consulting room about issues of gender, race, racism, power questions. It's sort of one thing to hear models presented that deal with all of this and another thing to say, well, how people are truly translating this into their practices. I don't know the answer to that.

Elaine: Right, especially in this day of managed care where there is so little time. And when you're dealing with all of these complexities, they take time to identify and to weave in whatever way that you're going to use them.

Lynn: Well, I think there are a number of people who are really struggling to do just that. As you know that is what my research is about–articulating just how therapists manage to intervene to impact power arrangements in their practice with couples and families. Actually, I found that the feminist family therapists I interviewed (and Evan you were one of them) are using very creative strategies for deliberately raising these difficult issues with clients who are either not aware of or necessarily interested in them. I have to say that I think these practitioners are the mavericks. They are certainly not the norm. Also, this perspective is sorely missing in most University and even family therapy curriculums. For example, I am disappointed that much of direct social work practice courses remain quite psychopathology oriented–missing the feminist and broader cultural perspectives that would seem such a natural fit. What do you see with the students you are training? Do you see these issues being addressed at Boston College, Elaine? Is it part of their curriculum?

Elaine: I have to answer that in several different ways. If you are talking about the curriculum, which is driven by the faculty, I would say that it is not where AFTA is at all. Feminism is there, and multiculturalism is there, and race on some level is there, but there isn't really an attempt to really deal with them together. They are presented in terms of theory and strategies. We don't have live supervision where students see colleagues at work and you can bring those issues in. Fortunately, certain groups of students are very interested in them. We actually have a live-wire group of students of color who got their own program together on working with diversity and families. They have brought in Janet Helms and people like that. It was amazing what they did. I also saw this at Hunter when I was there. So, some students are interested and they are aware. Others are not interested and could not care less.

Evan: Your point, Elaine, is an extremely important one, pedagogically–that as long as this material is taught as some separate thing . . .

Lynn: It is kind of an add on?

Evan: Yes. Or even if not an add on, but it is still seen as . . .

Elaine: Theoretical. Not service connected.

Evan: Yes, not service connected, not fully integrated into every single case that somebody is going to think through in terms of the questions that are raised in supervision and the questions that one asks oneself about a particular case. Until that really happens, I think we've moved forward, but not enough.

Elaine: There has to be time, and that's what we don't have.

Evan: And that's the other thing I was going to pick up on, and that was your comment about managed care. The thing that I really worry about, especially for new trainees, is that as they are being inducted into a very different kind of world of what it means to do therapy–that these issues seem superfluous or luxurious somehow, and that this isn't the real thing that we have to deal within three sessions.

Lynn: I agree, and yet if we believe power issues are not only central to the issues for which people come to therapy, but also warrant addressing in and of themselves, it seems we must be vigilant in our efforts both with clients we see and the students we train to help them to see they are the real thing. I think, as you imply, that we need to also take a stand against patriarchal systems (like managed care) that tend to bolster rather than challenge the status quo–the power inequities. As you point out, that is not easy to do in today's climate. Our students at the University of Denver are saying that what they are hearing from the practice community and faculty is that they need extensive training in the DSM, whatever it is now, IV? They are still being inducted into being very infatuated with pathology models.

Evan: Right.

Lynn: And so, they are demanding courses in that.

Evan: Precisely. Yes. So, in a way I think we are at a very dangerous moment where a lot of the gains could quickly be lost, I think, if we don't keep our eye on some of these government and social policy issues as to how is therapy going to be practiced, how is it going to be reimbursed, who is going to get therapy, and how do we continue deepening the awareness of multicultural issues, race, and gender in a time when people are being told to identify the symptom and dispatch it with Prozac.

Elaine: Prozac doesn't know race or gender, right? (Laughter)

Lynn: That's for sure! Do you see power politics in the family therapy field?

Elaine: Could you elaborate the question a little bit?

Lynn: I was just wondering, has our field, whether it is social work or family therapy, escaped power politics? Have we escaped political power positioning and competitiveness with one another–prestige in the field? (Laughter)

Evan: No is the answer to that question! And, I would add to that too that among women there, of course, has been competition and jockeying for position. I mean, how could there not be? I think when human beings get together and there is status and there is some version of fame and stuff like that, there is going to be competition and all of that. Now, how it plays out I guess is the question. And, it goes back to Elaine's point earlier about this somewhat crazy notion of a zero sum game that there is only so much power that can go around rather than the idea that when you start to share power, there is, in fact, more of it.

Elaine: Right.

Lynn: Elaine, you said earlier that when someone has power, they don't especially want to give it up.

Elaine: It's because they do not appreciate the point that Evan just made; there is no recognition of the possibility that there can be a different level of empowerment, broader and more substantive. I think the problem has to do with a personal need for power too as a way of–and this is my own idea–managing anxiety and discomfort, and not being able to use a shared power, a collaborative kind of stance, as a way of feeling empowered. Instead it is seen as a loss.

Lynn: Do you see women as being different than men once they are in power?

Elaine: Theoretically, certainly they should be because the stance that women have had has been less competitive and more relational and more interactional. But, I think they can get into it too.

Lynn: In the family therapy or social work fields, are there certain voices that are privileged over other voices? I am wondering if the feminist influence that you've talked about with AFTA is revealed in terms of whose work gets published, and that sort of thing.

Evan: I think it does more and more. Again, one of the things that the feminist critique within family therapy and the whole movement of women going back to the first Stonehenge Conference in 1984 where there was a deliberate organizing move on trying to get more women on the journal board, for instance, as well as at the beginning of this very journal, the *Journal of Feminist Family Therapy* started to make a difference so that more work, both by women and about these issues, could get published. I think one of the things that started to happen, and is still continuing to happen in certain quarters, is women helping other women in a mentoring kind of effort–so that women who don't quite understand what it means to send in a journal article, how to prepare it, or any of this crazy business, or even breaking into larger publishing of books, are getting some help from other women.

Lynn: Do you see it the same way Elaine?

Elaine: Yes, I think that's true. I think it hasn't happened as much in terms of people of color, but it is beginning to. AFTA has done well with that–of having articles published in their newsletter by people of color. I don't know how *Family Process* is doing.

Evan: Again, I think if you look at the journal board of *Family Process*, and also of *Journal of Marriage and Family Therapy*, there have been some increases. Again, I would say, not enough, but it was something that many people on those journal boards started to take very seriously and push for in some organized efforts that have made some changes.

Lynn: Are those people being used on the editorial board? Are they being sent articles?

Evan: Oh, yes, to the best of my knowledge, yes.

Elaine: I just want to say that the editor of the *Journal of Marriage and Family Therapy* is a woman, and it is Froma Walsh. There hasn't been a female editor of *Family Process* has there?

Evan: Not yet, no. (Laughter)

Elaine: I haven't seen a substantive number of articles on race or people of color in *Family Process*.

Evan: True.

Lynn: More so in the *Journal of Marriage and Family Therapy*?

Elaine: I'm not sure. It's my impression that there has been, but I may be wrong about that.

Lynn: Are there voices or issues that you think are considered fringe or missing in the field?

Evan: I'm not sure what you mean?

Lynn: Are there people or issues considered to be somehow not as legitimate, or more marginal? Perhaps that would be another way to say it.

Elaine: I don't quite know how to answer that. I think that everyone was marginalized except for one group, and we've been saying that there has been steady progress. It's not enough, but it has been changing. I would certainly like to see more articles by people of color in those two journals we just mentioned. I don't know about what kind of active planning they have done for that, or whether there is even much interest.

Evan: Exactly. To the best of my knowledge I don't think there is any kind of deliberate affirmative outreach for those kinds of articles. It is sort of two things. It is both articles about these issues and articles by people of color on any issues having to do with family therapy.

Elaine: But some journals will have special issues on these issues, but I've not seen much in these journals.

Evan: Right. What I did see recently, in terms of the issue of marginalized voices and things shifting, is there is going to be a big conference in San Francisco that Laura Markowitz is sponsoring through her magazine, *In the Family*, on gay and lesbian issues in therapy. I think this is the first time there has been a conference of this size. Previously there has been content within AMFT meetings, AFTA meetings, or *Networker* meetings. But, this will be an entire meeting devoted to these issues. So, I think that is another signal. Laura said in her introduction to writing about this conference, she was hearing more and more from people feeling there wasn't enough of this kind of content at the *Networker* meeting, so she decided to make a whole meeting.

Elaine: I would agree that gay and lesbian issues have been marginalized. Certainly, when you then look at the poor and people of color and gay and lesbians, there is nothing.

Lynn: Right.

Evan: I think the whole issue of poverty (something we haven't addressed so far in this conversation)–it goes back to what we were talking about regarding what is happening in the therapy field. I certainly have a great deal of concern (and I know Elaine shares this) as to what is happening in the public sector in terms of just front-line therapy/family therapy and the delivery of services to people who desperately need them. What kind of training are we doing for people to be able to do this kind of work? These are big questions to me.

Lynn: Elaine, and for you too?

Elaine: Absolutely, a great concern. If you look at the history of, certainly social work, it validates what Evan said. When we have certain hard times and when the climate shifts politically, then these forward movements that have gathered momentum and looked so promising, get silenced, or at least get blocked for a while.

Evan: That's right. People hunker down and they get worried about how they are going to make a living, and these issues that we've been talking about are then considered "fringe."

Elaine: And so managed care is acting like the depression did a while back, and it's very scary.

Lynn: How critical do you both think it is to incite family therapy with diversity issues? For example, to include issues of diversity in the therapy room even with clients who are not presenting those issues for themselves as problematic, like issues of racism, sexism, homophobia?

Elaine: Now, are you talking about clients whose connections are in those areas?

Lynn: Not necessarily, no–I mean with all clients. Do you think it is important, even with clients who are not talking about these issues as being the issues for which they have come to therapy? How critical do you think it is for the therapist to raise these issues in some way or another?

Elaine: I personally can't see how you could do that and have a client come back unless it was connected with his or her problem.

Evan: There has to be a connection. What I don't think is that therapy is a forum for our presenting our viewpoints that are not in the service of what the client is bringing. Now, many times people may not be identifying these as an issue, and the therapist starts to see ways that they are. That is different than, shall we say, "speechifying." Many times I will be working with people and there will be class issues that they have never identified, class differences between a husband and a wife, for instance. And, I do see that as my role to bring that to their awareness, and for us to talk about the meanings of that. Obviously, I think the gender differences in a heterosexual couple is a more obvious thing to be able to go for. It becomes more difficult for me, I think, if people are coming in and not identifying any issues of diversity as anything that is part of their terrain. Now, that is different from, for instance, if I hear racist comments. That, I will not be complicit with. Is that kind of the same for you, Elaine?

Elaine: Exactly. For me, of course, it is almost always there because I am a person of color no matter whom I am working with, and so that is why my vantage point is a little different–because it is always there.

Lynn: Do you think that your being a person of color makes it more necessary as well as perhaps easier to raise the issue?

Elaine: Certainly, it makes it–it's there. It needs to be addressed, especially if it's in the way, or if it's connected to the issues that the client is bringing, whether it is in terms of relationships or the problem that he or she has. I frequently use it particularly in terms of connecting to context because that seems to be a way to build a relationship and using it conveys such understanding of the complexity of the problem. It's always there for me; I might not always bring it up, but it's certainly always on my mind.

Lynn: This is what Rhea Almeida is attempting to do with clients that come to see her, and she does it in a very interesting way.

Elaine: Yes. She does it in a group, and that is a lot different.

Evan: Which I think makes for some other possibilities, more possibilities than you would have, for instance, when you are working with a couple or alone with an individual.

Elaine: Or even with a family.

Lynn: Yes, something about the groups, along with the various forms of therapy and social and political-education they do there, allows for a vivid sense of accountability that is harder to pull off with more traditional conceptualizations of therapy and settings. I think this is an area feminist family therapists need to address even though it is difficult. It is the rare family that will identify broader social issues as part of the reasons for which they seek therapy. Yet to not address the issues is to be in compliance with them.

Elaine: I'm not going to say that down the road there might not be a way to do it that would be very catalyzing and very useful. I'm not saying that, it's just that I don't see it at the moment.

Evan: I would agree with you, Elaine.

Lynn: Thanks to you both. I'm glad we finally made it happen.

INTERVIEW

Sukie Magraw, Interview Editor

An Interview
with Lillian Comas-Diaz, PhD

Lillian Comas-Diaz is the author of many articles; the founder and editor of the journal, *Culture Diversity and Mental Health*; and the co-editor, with Bev Greene, of the book, *Women of Color: Integrating Ethnic and Gender Identities into Psychotherapy.* She works at the Transcultural Mental Health Institute in Washington, DC.

This interview is in two parts: The first consists of excerpts from an interview conducted in 1993; the second is a follow-up interview conducted four years later.

Sukie Magraw, PhD, is Assistant Professor of Clinical Psychology in the PsyD Program at JFK University.

Address correspondence to Sukie Magraw at PsyD Program, JFK University, 12 Altarinda Road, Orinda, CA 94563.

[Haworth co-indexing entry note]: "An Interview with Lillian Comas-Diaz, PhD." Magraw, Sukie. Co-published simultaneously in *Journal of Feminist Family Therapy* (The Haworth Press, Inc.) Vol. 10, No. 1, 1998, pp. 113-129; and: *Transformations of Gender and Race: Family and Developmental Perspectives* (ed: Rhea V. Almeida) The Haworth Press, Inc., 1998, pp. 113-129. Single or multiple copies of this article are available for a fee from The Haworth Document Delivery Service [1-800-342-9678, 9:00 a.m. - 5:00 p.m. (EST). E-mail address: getinfo@haworthpressinc.com].

113

11/3/93

SM: Let me start by asking you how you became involved in the field of family therapy?

LCD: Basically, when I was doing my internship, I found that the techniques I was being taught–both individual and group therapy–were not sufficient. They were not bringing in one of the most important contexts in people's lives which is their family. That's how I got interested. Also, in my particular case, because I was working with an inner city population, I found the work of Minuchin quite helpful in conceptualizing and applying therapy with a lot of the clients I was seeing at that point.

SM: How did you end up in the field of psychology to begin with?

LCD: Well, I'm one of those people who when I was a child the other children would come and tell me their problems. So I said, "Gee, something is here." Now it's interesting that it was psychology because at that point I felt psychology was a blend of science and art. I guess that's still how I see therapy. I got interested in helping people but also keeping in mind the scientific basis of behavior. I thought it was a pretty good field that would be very comprehensive. So once I decided that people were coming to me for advice, I said, "Well, maybe I should become a psychologist."

SM: Was your decision supported in your family and by your friends?

LCD: This was way back. I was in elementary school.

SM: You decided at that age!?

LCD: Oh yes. I was about maybe 7 or 8.

. . .

SM: Where did you grow up? Where did you go to grade school?

LCD: I was born in Chicago. I went to Puerto Rico when I was about six years old. So I schooled there through high school and then college. Then I came here to the States.

SM: For graduate school?

LCD: I did a master's in Puerto Rico in psychology. I came to the States because I wanted to do a Ph.D. I ended up working for two years in a mental health program. Then I went to school at the University of Massachusetts and got a Ph.D.

SM: Why did your family move from Chicago to Puerto Rico?

LCD: First if you know something about Puerto Ricans, it's very common to move back and forth. Now what is not done very commonly, is that my parents stayed in the States and I moved to Puerto Rico where my grandparents were; I'm the oldest in my family. My parents stayed in the States for about four or five more years, then they moved back to the island. Going back to the issue of family therapy, it's interesting because staying with my maternal grandparents at that time, I had the extended family. We were sharing one house, upstairs and downstairs, with my aunt and her children. It was very ethnic.

SM: During that period would your parents come to visit?

LCD: Oh yeah. This was done for financial reasons. My parents are working class. They left the island because they couldn't find work. They came to the States with the classic immigrant story: no English, no nothing, working two jobs, sometimes three jobs, so they could earn a living.

SM: Did you have younger siblings who stayed in the States?

LCD: Yes. I have a brother who is four years younger than I am. He stayed with them. Then when they returned to Puerto Rico, about four years after I left, he, of course, came with them.

SM: That's interesting.

LCD: Well, when we talk about feminism you're going to hear why I think it's very interesting.

SM: We can put that in now if you're willing.

LCD: There were the two children in the family. Some Latino cultures and some Puerto Rican families value males quite a lot. My father was very invested in his son—not that he was not invested in me, but because I was a female I could handle being left with my grandparents and they would take good care of me. But for the boy that is a little different story. And by the way this is a very common story—that the preference is for the male.

SM: So it was easier for your parents to have you go back to Puerto Rico because you were a girl.

LCD: Maybe. We both went there. But my father said that because my brother was younger and he missed him, he returned. And I was older and handling the adjustment better. That's the story.

SM: I see. So your brother came back to the States. That sounds very difficult. Did you have hard feelings about it at the time?

LCD: I don't remember having hard feelings. If you compare Chicago to Puerto Rico there is a very big difference, especially in the winter. But for me it was very liberating to be in Puerto Rico because I started to grow up with my cousins and doing a lot of things: not being so restricted, having a more "normal" childhood. Playing games, doing all the things that you cannot do when you live in an inner city in the United States.

SM: So why did your parents go back to Puerto Rico?

LCD: They made enough money to buy a house, which is what they wanted to do. They always wanted to go back. That's the main reason they came here. I mean they were some of the few to be able to do that. I guess they were lucky. Because it was for financial reasons, issues of class are very close to my heart.

. . .

SM: How were you received and perceived as a Puerto Rican woman doing therapy?

LCD: Well, I guess by people who were interested in ethnicity and culture I was perceived very, very well. There were people who thought culture was not important, but let's say they had a patient, and if I came in as a consultant and they could see that what I was suggesting "made sense" and had an effect on the patient, then they would start acting differently.

SM: So, are you saying that otherwise there was an indifference towards you?

LCD: Indifference, and if you're working in inner cities, you're perceived as not that good. That may not be a reaction to family therapy, it may be a reaction to class or working with second class citizens.

. . .

SM: Did the women's movement have an effect on the way you did therapy?

LCD: Of course. Because I am dealing with different conceptualizations of what is feminism and what is sexism, I need to clarify that.

SM: OK.

LCD: For instance the type of sexism that we have in Latin America, or Puerto Rico particularly, is somewhat different from the type of sexism we have here.

SM: In what way?

LCD: Well, the type of sexism I encounter in Latin America is that women are not treated as equals. But that thinking is more linked to certain areas. It's not that women don't have brains; it's not related to intellectual inferiority. It's related to, "You have to do my meals, and you have to be the servant. And if you get a high position, you have to work but, in addition, you have to do X, Y, and Z." I mention that because my first contact with feminism, although intellectually I was in favor of it because I read a lot of it, when I started to see what White middle class and upper middle class were calling feminism I had difficulties with that.

SM: In what way?

LCD: It was not inclusive. It was basically what I just said, White, middle and upper class. So I had some difficulties with that. And I still do obviously. But what I did was not throw out the baby with the bath water. By being bi-cultural or multi-cultural, you need to integrate a lot, and some things you don't integrate because you feel comfortable with that. So I could integrate some areas, and other areas I kept them quite separate, yet co-existent. Am I making sense?

SM: Yes.

LCD: Feminism was very influential when it moved into therapy, into family therapy, and even though it was not totally inclusive, it was less exclusive than the mainstream type of therapy that I was used to studying and doing. Of course the whole list of why empowerment orientations are important for women and for people of color made a lot of sense to me. I saw feminist therapy as quite congruent with some of the tenets of family therapy in terms of the importance of the context, not pathologizing, empowering people, and encouraging social action outside the therapeutic hour or therapeutic encounter. This is not something that you do in a one shot deal; this is how you live. So I found those things, from my perspective, quite consistent. Now, of course, some traditional family therapists are very sexist, or if not, they reinforce some sexist positions in society. I'm well aware of that. That's why the field of feminist family therapy is so important right now in trying to address those issues. And I feel somewhat comfortable, not where we are, but that we have been moving. For awhile it was very bad; family therapy was dominated by a lot of men. I'm not saying that's bad, but usually these people did not challenge a lot of things that were beneficial to the male. Why give up power?

SM: Are you making a distinction between feminism and addressing sexism?

LCD: Yes. I think you heard me correctly. Let me tell you what my full thought is. Feminism may address some types of sexism, but other types of "isms" are not being addressed. For instance the "isms" of women of color, or the "isms" of lesbians, or the "isms" of aging women. When I think about feminism I think about being more empowering, trying to equalize relationships between people, and discussing the issues of power and control.

SM: So empowerment of all oppressed groups?

LCD: Or empowerment of people who are not oppressed. There are people in the mainstream who may be privileged by virtue of X, Y, and Z, but these people maybe have so-called "internalized domination," and in a way that's oppressive because it limits the way you see reality. If you see members of this particular group as being inferior, you're not even aware of it but you go about your business like that, you are limiting yourself. So what I'm saying is that I see empowerment for all people. I'm extending the definition of oppression because sometimes you can be oppressed in your mind even though you have a lot of privilege in society.

. . .

SM: What about the influence of other civil rights movements on you? Were you here in the States during the 60s?

LCD: No, but I read all about it. That was extremely important for me. As a Puerto Rican woman, I'm a mixed race woman. It's a long story and I'm not going to fill your tape with it. In terms of racism in the Caribbean, racism is alive and well. It takes different shapes and forms. Some people want to say that in Latin America racism is more associated with class, which is true. If you go to Latin America the people who have more tend to be White looking or European looking. Now, why am I saying that? Because when we talk about the determination of what racial group we belong to, we're not talking simply about Black and White; we're talking about the whole gamut of racial determinations according to how your hair is, what color you are, the nose, the shape, what look you have. You can be mulatto, you can be Indian, you can be Greek. . . . It's like the Eskimos and snow, they have about 12 words for different kinds of snow. That's what it's like. The only thing I can think that would be closer in an American nomenclature would be in New Orleans with the quadroon, or the octoroon, and hectoroon, all those denominations. We have the same thing in the Caribbean and parts of Latin America.

So, racially in Puerto Rico, I am seen as non White. I'm not seen as black Black, but I'm seen as non White. Let's put it this way, I'm seen as mixed Black. So when I came to the States I had a dual identification. One was obviously the Hispanic and the Latina. And the other was the African American. So, the civil rights movement was very important to me. I got here right in the midst of it; I was wearing my afro. I felt a lot of solidarity with the African American group.

SM: Were you accepted at that time by both the Hispanic and African American groups?

LCD: I cannot tell you how I was accepted by the African American group. I can tell you that I was seeing a lot of clients who were African American and they stayed with me. They had the option of seeing someone else. So that affected me very much because I was able to have access to peers and clients and communities that if I had stayed in my Hispanic/Latino community I would have been more protected but I would not have been able to grow and have a wider political perspective.

SM: Was that wider perspective available to you in the United States in a way that it was not available to you in Puerto Rico?

LCD: Yes. If you're Black that type of discrimination is very different from the one here because the one there is more covert.

SM: In Puerto Rico it's more covert?

LCD: Yes, but it's there.

SM: And is that mixed with class?

LCD: Absolutely. Here if you're Black, you're Black, you're Black. So the color situation is more fluid in Latin America. Anyway, because of those experiences I was able to open myself to be more receptive and to see the impact of the civil rights. I was permeable to that, and of course it affected me and it affected my work.

. . .

SM: How have feminist issues affected your life personally?

LCD: Well, I've always been very concerned about gender socialization and been very critical–in terms of analysis–of gender socialization

of people. As you know, because of my own personal history, you
see a clear demarcation in roles and expectations just because of
gender. I have been very interested in understanding traditional
Latino sex roles because my mother is very traditional and my
father as well. I saw the effect that had on me and my brother. And
at the same time I had a grandmother who was very feminist.

SM: Is that right?

LCD: She would not call herself feminist or anything. In the Latin culture
we have a gender role called "hembrismo" which basically means
female. It relates to the central role that females used to have among
the Indians and the central role of the Black female who was a slave
who came to the island. So I started to write about integrating these
two ideas. Here you have a society that is very traditional and a
gender role about a woman who is very submissive and passive, and
then you have another gender role of a woman who is very active
and proactive. So thinking about gender has been with me since the
very beginning, and how the relationship can be equalized and how
people get discriminated against by gender. I think my experience
helped me to understand firsthand people who were discriminated
against because of class and color, and in other areas as well.

11/18/97

LCD: After we spoke last time, I came out of the racial closet. I wrote an
article in which I coined a term, "Latinegra" or "Latinegro" which
is basically addressing the African Latino perspective. But in Spanish, when you say Africano Latino you are denying the Latin aspect
of being a black Latino. The article talks about all of these issues,
how this is a segment of the population and how this oppression is
at so many different levels.

But let's go on. What else did you want to ask me about?

SM: I want to ask you about your current work and about being the
editor of *Cultural Diversity and Mental Health*.

LCD: That's right. When I talked to you last we were not doing that. Well,
as I reread that interview I see that I was telling you that I was ready
to get into doing other things to balance my life and do more
creative things in a more expressive way. Then I ended up founding
and editing a new journal, *Cultural Diversity and Mental Health*. So
much for my predictions.

SM: Tell me about your journal.

LCD: It is an interdisciplinary journal. The opportunity presented itself and I grabbed it and ran with it. It has been one of the most interesting and challenging things I have done professionally.

SM: In what ways?

LCD: It has made me use a lot of my skills as a scholar, as a researcher, and as a politician, because it is very much a political statement. I see myself as an orchestra director because I have to orchestrate all these different manuscripts into a symphony (hopefully). It has been very challenging and fascinating; it has been very labor intensive but at the same time it has been very rewarding.

SM: Now you have been the editor for several years, haven't you?

LCD: Since '94.

SM: Also since I talked to you last, your edited book, *Women of Color*, has come out with Bev Greene.

LCD: When I talked to you last time we were just delivering the book. Since then, so many wonderful things have happened. After that Bev has come up with the book on gays and lesbians of color. It's wonderful; there has been an explosion of cultural diversity books compared to the way it used to be. So yes, it has been very rewarding to continue to work in this area. I think that even since the last time we spoke, issues of culture and race, class, ethnicity, and sexual orientation, are really more and more present in the mainstream.

SM: The fact that these issues are more in the mainstream, what effect has that had on how therapy is conducted?

LCD: Well, more people are getting trained, there are more books out there, and therapists are saying, "I need continuing education credits in working with diverse populations." The regular media is dealing more with it. The DSM-IV came out with the cultural axis to do cultural formulations. I know a lot of psychologists criticize it but I think it's great because it is placing culture in mainstream mental health. A lot of the political work I did for the journal was to get the experts in culture and psychiatry to be consulting editors for the journal. These are the people who are making the agenda for cultural psychiatry right now, and are writing the cultural for mental health diagnosis and treatment. I think the field is moving extremely well. The effect is that people are no longer seeing culture as an adjunct. You have to get training in it. Anyone who uses the DSM-IV has to know what a cultural formulation is. Also, in training, people are now getting more exposure to it. Right now I just got the galley proofs of our next journal issue. One of the articles is by a White, Jewish, gay man talking about his experiences with a black woman who was his family's maid, coming to terms with his own racism. This was the master's thesis of this psychology student! So, therapists are examining more how their culture interacts with their client's culture.

SM: How do you think family therapy is doing as a field with these issues?

LCD: Several years ago family therapy was in the vanguard because a lot of family therapists are social workers, and a lot of social workers have been trained in issues around culture and class–all of those issues. I think in my previous interview I mentioned Minuchin and Bowen. In fact, as outsiders within diverse contexts, a lot of Jewish Latin Americans have been involved in coining parts of the family therapy movement. I was thinking about Minuchin and Madanes and Celia Falicov. Five or ten years ago I would have said family therapists were in the vanguard. Now what I think is happening with family therapy–and this is not a criticism of family therapy per se–is that it has gotten "too established." Any field once it gets established, gets too comfortable and it becomes "them" instead of "us." The same thing is happening with feminist therapy.

SM: Can you say more?

LCD: Well, when you have a new field, developmentally speaking, that is trying to get known, that feels it has something new to say, there is a lot of resistance to it, and everybody gets galvanized and unionized. There is a feeling that we need to challenge the system. When the field is at that stage everyone is a member of the family; some are more favored than others; some are more stepchildren. But once the field becomes part of the mainstream, people start getting too comfortable. Was it Gloria Steinem who said that "Feminism made women become the men they wanted men to be." Similarly, that's my interpretation of what is going on with family therapy generally. There's still a lot of good stuff being done. But we are starting to suffer from group-think behavior and not pushing more of the limits, and not questioning established rules or ourselves. That's why the feminist part of always examining yourself and developing more of a consciousness is the way to go.

So, I don't know what else I can tell you. One of the difficulties with feminist therapy is the whole thing about white feminists thinking that the most important thing is gender, regardless of class and color. Then feminists of color say, "We believe in feminism but we need to add shades." For many people it may not be gender; for many people it is race and gender. That's part of the dilemma of what we were talking about earlier with feminists of color dealing with white feminists and the whole issue of the relationship to men of color. Gender is not the prevailing force. It is a combination of the culture, race, ethnicity, gender, class. Anna Castillo said it beautifully in *Massacre of the Dreamers*: "While I have more in common with a Mexican man than a white woman, I have much more in common with an Algerian woman than I do a with a Mexican man."

SM: That is great. What about this whole issue of men of color?

LCD: Men of color are not exempt from being sexist. They may be sexist but it may take a different shape and form, but sexism is there. Sometimes it is more the internalization of oppression in that, "I, as a man of color, have limited power in this society. The only arena in which I have power is in my home. I am a heterosexual man, so my control area has to be my family: my wife and my children." Sometimes the boundaries get blurred so the oppression from the outside gets internalized into oppression from the inside. People who are traumatized tend to traumatize their loved ones or other people. This can lead to domestic violence. We have a whole issue coming up [In *Cultural Diversity and Mental Health*] that focuses on domestic violence in communities of color. This is a serious problem. One problem that we have is that we do not want to air our dirty laundry in public. People will say, "They're as bad as we thought; they're even worse." A lot of women of color present an appearance that everything is fine when everything is not fine because we are concerned about consequences. If, for instance, there is a family of color where there is incest, the kids are going to be taken away immediately, particularly if they are a low income family of color. Whereas if it were a white family of a certain class there might be therapy, or some other intervention. There is a criminalization of behavior according to racial differences. That makes it difficult to air our dirty laundry in public.

SM: So this journal issue makes a bold statement.

LCD: Yes. But those of us who are clinicians are seeing people in our offices whose lives are being destroyed by this. We need to do something about it. We just cannot continue with this political perspective alone. We need to talk to each other and to borrow skills from other fields like trauma therapy on how to address these issues. Talking and being compassionate about it, being researchers, we need to figure out and examine the best ways to deal with these problems. We have a major responsibility. Am I making sense?

SM: Yes. Before we started taping you were saying that there is a level of comfort you would have talking about all of these shades with other women of color that you would not have with women of non-color.

LCD: And, why is that?

SM: Yes. Can you speak to that?

LCD: First of all, we live in the reality. We [women of color] are not going to necessarily pathologize or criminalize that reality. Even white people who are well intended, who are feminists, just by being a member of class of people who have some type of oppression, but not this type of oppression, is going to–the whole issue of privilege–make you look at it from a different perspective unless you are examining yourself, doing some anti-racism work, liberating yourself, that type of thing. Being aware of what are your Achilles' heels. I'm very good at telling who is racist against Latinas but I may not be as good at telling who is racist against Asians. Or, I might pick up somebody who is racist but I may not pick up somebody who is homophobic. So, I'm not sure; I don't trust myself that much. My tendency, to use an overused phrase, is to be culturally paranoid. As women of color we need to protect our group, our family. And we are all members of the family, no matter how many differences we have. Latinos, we have so many differences between ourselves: Puerto Ricans, Cubans, Mexicans, South Americans of color. The same thing with Asians. But we are all members of the family when we are dealing with the mainstream. Some people would not agree with me, but that is the way I see it.

SM: I am thinking of the last interview that we did and you were maintaining that we are all oppressed.

LCD: But "some oppressions are different from others," to paraphrase George Orwell's *Animal Farm*.

SM: Yes. Can you flesh that out a little bit?

LCD: Let me give you a clinical example I use in the book. Let's say there is a therapist who was raped who has recovered successfully. She is working with a Vietnamese woman who was raped. Those two oppressions are not the same. If the therapist assumes that she has gone through the same experience, this can be very unfortunate and destructive to the patient if she assumes that all oppressions traumatize equally.

When I mentioned that to you last time, we all feel that we have been oppressed in certain ways: This is one of the exercises we use to sensitize people to differences. But this is a way of building a connection. It is not to say that we all are the same.

SM: It's a way of having some common humanity, that we all have experiences of pain and hurt.

LCD: Exactly. Again this is all culturally specific. Right now, we may see someone who has lost their whole family; that's really trauma. Maybe in the future it will be something else. It is very specific to the context.

SM: You mention trauma work a lot and I know in the past you have worked with victims of torture. Can you say more about that.

LCD: In most of my work, particularly the work I do with people who are different, I borrow a lot from trauma. For example, some types of sexism, some types of racism are really traumas.

SM: How would you distinguish those types that are from those that aren't?

LCD: It would be hard to put this in a "recipe" because everything is so subjective. Not being invited to the senior prom, now that we are in our 40s or 50s, we say, "Gee, you were traumatized at that age." So everything is subjective. But I think it has to do with enduring scars that really change the way you see yourself and the way you see the world. It is an identity transformer. One of the things I do, in which my cognitive behavioral theoretical background is very useful, has to do with assessing level of functioning. How I see myself functioning, how my significant others see me functioning. This is an area which I am still in process of conceptualizing. When I see a woman from Guatemala who has seen members of her family tortured, it is just something completely different.

SM: Completely different from the prom.

LCD: Yes, different levels.

SM: Some people, like Maria Root, I believe, make the argument that racism is traumatic.

LCD: Many people are holding that belief right now, that racism is trauma. At least in my experience, I have found myself using a lot of the skills I use in working with trauma victims when I see people of color and they present with racism. It's the same thing with sexual abuse. It was not an issue because people didn't ask. I'm not saying therapy should just be how many times you have been victimized by racism or sexism, but this is people's lives, this is how they present, and we have to address it. And we have to be much more culturally specific. The way I would see, let's say a Latin American person who has been through political oppression, is very different from how I would work with, let's say an Ethiopian. And don't ask me the difference!

SM: OK.

LCD: Let's go back to Rhea's mandate for this discussion. I think there's the issue of not trusting completely the system.

SM: Which system?

LCD: The general system. For instance, the Anita Hill situation, many people including myself, refused to comment publicly. It would be pitting a woman of color against a man of color. We do that all the time, but publicly, no. The APA Monitor wanted to interview me and other people, but we said, "No." We talked a lot among ourselves, but we were not sure how the mainstream was going to use that. There's a deficit orientation. The dialogue becomes a focus on those African-Americans or those Latinos or whomever. We become the targets of all kinds of projections. The society as a whole is not ready to see people of color as people. We're objects.

SM: Did you feel similarly about the O.J. Simpson case, that you did not want to comment?

LCD: That's a tough one. It did not involve pitting a man of color against a woman of color. I did some media interviews in which I talked about domestic abuse and how that could kill. I was interviewed on CNN in Spanish and NBC in Spanish. A lot of women contacted me afterwards to discuss domestic violence. We need to talk about this in our communities because otherwise it will continue. We need to do it a way that women can hear it and that they become more empowered, not disempowered, and that it doesn't become a witch trial.

Let me give you another recent example. The only person I've talked to about this is my husband. Louise Woodward. Remember, she is British.

SM: Yes.

LCD: You remember the ethnicity of the father of the baby?

SM: No.

LCD: He is Indian, from India.

SM: I didn't know that.

LCD: That baby is mixed race. Now, what is the relationship between white British and Indians in England?

SM: Ahh. Britain colonized India.

LCD: It is similar dynamics or even worse than whites and blacks here. Worse because they were colonized and they didn't have the civil rights movement that we had here. So, one of the reasons this young woman may have treated this kid the way she did was because he was not totally human in her eyes. He was an Indian. I'm not sure this guy was Indian, he may be Pakistani, but he is from the colonized subcontinent. Nobody has mentioned this. I can't believe it!

That is why this is such a hard topic. All of these things are operating on so many different levels. That's why the paranoia is always there. Let's face it, some of my esteemed colleagues would not be doing this interview with you. And I have to respect their decisions.

SM: Yes. I have had some of your colleagues turn me down for interviews. They did not trust that they would be fairly represented. I was unhappy with that, but I had to respect it.

LCD: I did these interviews because maybe my political views are a little different, and like Rhea, I come from a colonized country, so I see the realities from a little bit of a different perspective. Many times my colleagues and I agree on things, and sometimes we don't agree. They respect me and I respect them. I try to make a bridge and help the field move along. Sometimes I am successful, and sometimes I fail, becoming frustrated and unhappy. But having that political perspective helps me a lot to withstand the pressure I get from the whites and sometimes the pressure I get from my own community. Because then I don't personalize it as much.

SM: Talking of the pressure you sometimes get from your own community reminds me of Ken Hardy's idea of "psychological homelessness."

LCD: Exactly, look at my friend Bev Greene. She talks about lesbians and gays of color not being completely accepted within communities of color nor in the gay and lesbian communities. This topic is fraught with contradictions. For example, you have gays of color dying of AIDS, and they go home and are taken care of. Another friend, when her brother was dying of AIDS, she took a year off from her busy career to take care of him, to be with him. And she is representative of many women of color. No matter how religious and homophobic they are, they put away the bible, they forget about that and they take care of family. This is the kind of contradiction.

Being from a colonized country, I have to deal and live with contradiction; sometimes you integrate them, and sometimes you don't, and you live with it because life is like that.

SM: Can you give me an example from your life? This may be hard to do because it is so pervasive.

LCD: Exactly, it's like defining who I am. Well, I'll give you an example of a small one. It's not that I don't want to share more important ones with you, it's just that I don't want them published. Some years ago I worked at APA directing the Office of Ethnic Minority Affairs. At that time, believe me, culture, ethnicity and race were not in vogue. I was surrounded by the mainstream assumption that minorities are lazy, that they don't want to work, that they just want to come to Washington to sit and do nothing on these committees. Of course, this was a fallacy. These people were working! We had to always justify that the work we were doing was A-okay, that we were not wasting the money of the organization. And then, when I was turning to the Board of Ethnic Minority Affairs, I had to justify that I was not working for the man, that we were not slaves; they were suspicious about the agenda. There was that type of duality. And I had to understand that those were historical voices, that it was not that I was not doing a good job, but in that particular position, in that historical era, was going to be full of those type of issues. I was in the position of being the infamous Greek messenger.

SM: So you were caught between these two forces, having to forge your way. It sounds thankless.

LCD: Yes.

SM: We're coming to the end of our time. When I last interviewed you, you said you were going to cut back on your work, but now with your editorship you have failed miserably.

LCD: But I did hold the line to only one term of editorship.

SM: So, that's good.

LCD: And I am making space in my life to do other things, like I am attending more concerts, and I love movies and reading. So I am doing these things that are totally unrelated to work. Since you and I talked last, I have lost some members of my family and some have gotten very sick. That really humbles you. It makes you wake up and smell the roses.

SM: Really, I'm sorry to hear that.

LCD: Thank you. It's been tough, very tough. But at the same time you realize how lucky you are. This had made me see things a little bit differently. I'm getting a little more into the spiritual aspect of the work. This may be developmental; I'm 47 now. But I'm integrating that more into my work and I'm very pleased.

SM: Can you say more about that?

LCD: This would be a whole new interview! Let me just say that I'm looking at the connection of the mind, body and spirit from a cultural perspective. I have been studying spiritual beliefs and seeing how that dovetails with my work and also my own development.

SM: Thank you so much for talking to me again.

LCD: Thank you for this opportunity.

Index

ADHD, case example of, 42-43
African American children, racial
  identification of, 30-33
African American men
 case example of, 53
 masculinity differences in, 51,63
 in prisons, 8
African American women
 domestic violence and, 9-10
 in female-headed households, 6
 in labor force, 5
 maternal mortality rate of, 8
 single women percentages of, 6
AFTA (American Family Therapy
  Academy), 101-105,107,109
Almeida, Rhea, 1,3,7,8,9,12,52,85,86,
  88-92,99,111
American Family Therapy Academy
  (AFTA), 101-105,107,109
Asian Americans
  child-rearing practices of,
  29,40,42
 racial identification, of children
  and, 30
 women in labor force and, 5
Attention deficit hyperactive disorder.
  See ADHD
Autonomy, child development of,
  34-35

Bepko, Claudia, 52

Case examples
 of ADHD, 42-43
 of African American male
  relationships, 53

of diverse woman's experience,
  3,14-17,42-43
of dominant feminism, 9-10
of homosexual masculinity
  differences, 53
Child development
 addictions and, 40
 autonomy and self-determination,
  myth of, 34-35
 behavioral styles and, 37-39
 Bem's gender schema theory of, 30
 case example of, 42-43
 communication and, 23,24-26,33,
  37,40
 conclusions regarding, 43-44
 cultural consciousness of, 43-44
 cultural factors and, 8,23,25,27-29,
  30-31,33-34,35,36,38-42
 dominant culture and, 24,25,32,
  40-41
 dominant imaging in, 38
 Erickson's theories of human
  development and, 27-28
 Freud's childhood seduction
  theories and, 28
 gender factors in, 23,26,30,33-34,
  41
 gender gaps relative to, 30
 identities, in diversity context,
  41-42
 immigrant children and, 32-33
 intelligence potential in, 32
 interdependent self, development
  of, 35-42
 interdependence, within
  relationships context, 29,33,
  35,37-39
 language and, 26-29,32,37-39
 literature review on, 27-33

Journal of Feminist Family Therapy
(JFFT)
article review in, 4-5,12
evolution of, 3
Jung, Carl G., 24

Labor force, cultural diversity in, 5
Latino men, masculinity and, 52,54-55
Latino women, in labor force, 5
Lesbianism, women of color and,
2,14,128

Managed care
*Couple and Family in Managed
Care, The: Assessment,
Evaluation, and Treatment*
(Bagarozzi), 134-136
family therapy and, 104,106,109
Masculinity
cultural factors and differences of,
50,51-52,54,55-57,58-60
diversity case examples of, 53,
55-56,57
employment and, 14-17,51,56,58,
62-63
expanded norms of, 69,70,87,96
gender roles in, 52,54,55,74,76
homosexual differences in, 52,53,
54,55,58,63,68-71,75
ideals of, 69-70
men in movements and, 49,57,
140-142
military culture and, 51,52,54,
60-62,64-65,140-142
positive aspects of, 71-72,78
sexuality and, 14-17
toughness and, 83
traditional norms of, 51,70,
71,72,81-83,87
unemployment and, 16,62,73
Maturity
development of, 23-27,35
measurement of, 23-27,33-34,
36,43-44

See also Child development
Men of color
oppression of, 123
statistics on, 7-8,51,87
See also Cultural factors; Racial
factors; Women of color
Messineo, Theresa, 52
Military
masculinity concept differences
and, 51,52,54,60-62,64-65,
140-142
women in, 60-62,64-65,66

National Organization of Men Against
Sexism (NOMAS), 49-50,60
Native Americans
cultural tradition and, 42
women in labor force and, 5
Nazario, Andres, 52,53-57
NOMAS (National Organization of
Men Against Sexism),
49-50,60

Odim, Cheryl Johnson, 1

Pacific Islander women, in labor
force, 5
Parenting
discipline styles in, 8-9
racial factors in, 6,8-9,32,40-41
"shift" concept in, 6, 8
Piaget, Jean, 28
*Politics of Masculinities: Men in
Movements* (Messner),
140-142
Pornography, 15-17,52
Power
abuse of, 86-87
gender differences of, 2,41,87,
92,101
hierarchies of, 85,86,87
racial factors in, 12-13,23-27,
85-92,100

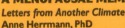